Mamuri Hearts

Enjoy the book

Danny Passu

Martial Hearts
The Defensive Mental Edge

By Danny Passmore

TATE PUBLISHING
AND ENTERPRISES, LLC

Martial Hearts
Copyright © 2016 by Danny Passmore. All rights reserved.

No part of this publication may be reproduced, stored in a retrieval system or transmitted in any way by any means, electronic, mechanical, photocopy, recording or otherwise without the prior permission of the author except as provided by USA copyright law.

This book is designed to provide accurate and authoritative information with regard to the subject matter covered. This information is given with the understanding that neither the author nor Tate Publishing, LLC is engaged in rendering legal, professional advice. Since the details of your situation are fact dependent, you should additionally seek the services of a competent professional.

The opinions expressed by the author are not necessarily those of Tate Publishing, LLC.

Published by Tate Publishing & Enterprises, LLC
127 E. Trade Center Terrace | Mustang, Oklahoma 73064 USA
1.888.361.9473 | www.tatepublishing.com

Tate Publishing is committed to excellence in the publishing industry. The company reflects the philosophy established by the founders, based on Psalm 68:11,
"The Lord gave the word and great was the company of those who published it."

Book design copyright © 2016 by Tate Publishing, LLC. All rights reserved.
Cover design by Samson Lim
Interior design by Mary Jean Archival

Published in the United States of America

ISBN: 978-1-68187-292-6
1. Self-Help / Personal Growth / General
2. Sports & Recreation / Martial Arts & Self-Defense
15.12.22

For Audrey

Acknowledgments

SPECIAL THANKS TO the following people: Karen, Becky, Aidan, Donovan, Riley, and Ryan. David and Sydney. Michael. Steven and Serena, Jay, Christine, Abigail, Gabriel, Isabel and Nathaniel. Kristi, Audrey, and all thirty board members of the Nice Ninjas.

Helpful Websites and Phone Numbers

Boundaries: A Guide for Teens
Girls and Boys Town
1-800-282-6657
www.girlsandboystown.org

W.A.I.T. Training
WAIT (why am I tempted)
720-488-8888

National 24 hour hotline
866-331-9474 or text Loveis to 22522
Loveisrespect.org
Break the Cycle – abuse support
www.breakthecycle.org

Federal Bureau of Investigation
Report on human trafficking
Young women abducted and sold into sex slavery
www.fbi.gov

Bureau of Justice Statistics
Reports on Rape and Sexual Assault
www.bjs.gov

Institute for American Values
www.americanvalues.org

National Hotline Numbers

Alcohol questions 800-662-4357
Alcoholic in your home 888-425-2666
Anxiety 866-615-6494 or 800-273-8255 or 855-581-8111
Bullying 855-581-8111 or text TALK to 85511
Child abuse 800-422-4453
Crime victims 866-689-HELP (4357)
Crisis call center 800-273-8255
Dating abuse for teens 866-331-9474
Deaf and hearing impaired TDD number for all hotlines 866-604-5350
Depression 630-482-9696 or 800-784-2433 or 800-442-4673
Domestic violence 800-799-SAFE (7233)
Drugs 800-662-4357 or 800-784-6776
Eating disorder 800-931-2237
Grief and Loss 800-959-8277 or 800-273-8255
Homeless and Runaway 800-448-3000 or 800-273-8255 or text ANSWER to 839863

Incest 800-799-7233

Parenting questions teenage 888-510-2229 or 800-448-3000 or 800-944-4773 (call usually returned within twenty-four hours)

Pregnancy 866-942-6466

Pregnancy teenage 866-942-6466 or 888-510-2229 or 800-550-4900

Rape 800-799-7233 or 800-656-4673

Runaway 800-RUNAWAY (786-2929)

School violence 800-273-8255 or 866-773-2587

Self-injury 800-366-8288

Sexual assault 800-656-4673 or 800-273-8255

Stress 866-615-6494 or 800-273-8255 or 855-581-8111

Suicide 800-784-2433 or 800-442-4673

Thursday's child national youth advocacy 800-972-5437

*Train up a child in the way he should go,
and when he is old he will not depart from it.*

—Ancient Proverb

About the Author

DANNY PASSMORE BEGAN his martial arts training on January 2, 1972 in Waco, Texas, under Dennis Gotcher. He retired from training and teaching in 2009, when his Marine Corps injuries prevented him from continuing any longer. Throughout his career, Mr. P (as his students affectionately called him) became known first for his work with the deaf, and later for his successful teaching of students with attention deficit hyperactivity disorder (ADHD) and other learning disabilities. He also coined the phrase, "The family that kicks together, sticks together," which has become a common phrase throughout the United States.

He was inducted into the World Martial Arts Hall of Fame as one of the last true pioneers in martial arts for his work with the Deaf after putting together an all-medaled deaf tae kwon do tournament team. Three of whom were promoted to black belt, and two of those went on to become tae kwon do masters. He then founded the Texas Martial Arts

Hall of Fame©, which still operates today. He also produced a television show entitled *Martial Arts Masters of Texas©*.

In the year 2000, Mr. P developed his *Nice Ninja©* program for at-risk children. His catchphrase was "training tomorrow's leaders today." Having taught behavioral skills to be an important part of self-defense training, Mr. P wrote and published his works on emotional self-defense entitled *Positive Defensive Behavior©* in 2006.

After his retirement, he completed this workbook, his second book in 2013. Retiring as a ninth-degree black belt, Grandmaster Passmore continues to draw his strength and perseverance from his relationship with God. He has survived terminal cancer (of the spleen, pancreas, and intestines), hepatitis, diabetes, a murder attempt, and a three-month false imprisonment for the false accusation of harming a child. After this ordeal, Mr. Passmore retired to the Texas coast near the beach he loved so much as a child.

Mr. P now spends his days touring the country by motorcycle, target shooting, and writing short stories for kids with reading deficiencies. Each story is from his personal adventures, from exploring a secret underground submarine base on the Italian coast to a fact-finding mission in the Sahara Desert where he trained the Polisario army.

Contents

Preface 23
Introduction: Ready, Fire, Aim 25
1   Life's Not a Hamburger, It's a Casserole 33
2   Who's in Charge Here? 41
    Section 1: Children 41
    Section 2: Youth 45
    Section 3: Preadults 46
3   Demons from the Id 47
4   Types of Thought 51
    Working Through Types of Thoughts 53
5   Planning Your Future 55
    A Study Guide for Young People of Any Age 55
    Organizing Your Backpack and Locker 61
    Organizing at Home 62
    Organizing at School 64

	Study Skills 67
	When You Get the Test 71
	Handling Long Study Sessions 72
	Things To Remember 74
6	Important Social Skills 79
	Disagreeing 80
	Accepting Criticism 83
	Compliments vs. Flattery 86
	Asking for Help 90
	Expressing Feelings Appropriately 92
	Following Instructions 95
	How to Accept Being Told No 104
	How to Express Empathy and Understanding of Others 108
	How to Apologize 110
	How to Accept an Apology 111
	Greeting Courtesy 112
	Phone Courtesy 117
	Car Courtesy 119
	Walking Courtesy 121
	Dining Courtesy 122
	Going Indoors 124
	Persons in Conversation 125
	School or Business 126
	Discourteous People 127

7	Basic Hygiene	129
8	Proper Breathing Techniques	133
9	The Difference Between Men and Women	137
	The Brain	138
	Emotions	139
	Sex	140
	Physiology	141
10	Relationships	143
11	Developing Healthy Relationships	149
12	Spirituality	153
13	Boundaries	155
	External Boundaries	156
	Internal Boundaries	156
	Boundaries of Space	156
14	Intimacy	163
15	Purity	165
16	The Brain Needs More, Not Less	167
	No Man Is an Island	169
17	Emotional Con Games	171
	Jealousy and Possessiveness	174
	Insecurity	177
	Intimidation	181
	Anger	183
	Accusations	188
	Flattery	189

	Status	191
	Bribery	195
	Control..	196
18	Teasing	199
19	Dating Self-Defense Techniques	203
	Hand on the Leg.....................................	204
	Arm Around the Shoulder	204
20	Other Self-Defense Moves.....................................	207
	How to Hold Your Keys in the Parking Lot..........	207
	Escapes from Grabs	208
	Strikes	212
21	Finding an Appropriate Martial Arts School...........	215
22	Stories...	221
	The Harp...	222
	Special Needs	223
	The White Suit Story	226
	My Greatest Christmas Gift	227
	The Fighting Wolves	229
	Unending Hurt of Drug Abuse.............................	230
	Texas Teen Hears Tae Kwon Do's Call...................	232
	My Last Rodeo	237
	What Experience Has Taught Me	241
	What Experience Has Taught Me Explained........	244

Appendix I	263
The Seven Deadly Sins	263
Department of Justice Figures	263
Office on Violence	265
Appendix II	267
Notes	274
Phone Numbers	275

Preface

ONE MORNING, WHILE watching television, a news story was reported that would change my life and the direction of my martial arts school. A small child named Dynadia Thompson had been kidnapped and murdered in a neighboring town. The last time she was seen alive was leaving school, riding on the shoulders of an older-looking man.

For the next two weeks, all I could think about was Dynadia Thompson. Finally it hit me. For years, people, fearing for the safety of their children, brought them to my self-defense school, and I taught them a sport. This had to change.

I immediately began seeking out other types of martial arts, which focused more on street tactics. Although most of them were used in a sport (such as judo), they all had applications that were effective on the street. The more I learned, the more techniques I implemented into my curriculum. I began inviting instructors to teach seminars with my students to strengthen the new direction of my school.

Eventually, our teaching became uniquely different than our traditional training, so we changed the name to American Street Karate. Other schools making the same transition joined with us, and together we began truly meeting the needs of those who wanted street defense. Then another life-changing news story caught my eye.

While reading "Dear Abby" in the local newspaper, I read an article from a young lady in Florida who needed help accepting a compliment. Her previous boyfriend had beat her down with emotional battering. He often told her how she was fat and ugly and no one would want her and how lucky she was to have him.

She eventually left him and had a new boyfriend who frequently complimented her beauty and kindness toward others, but she couldn't believe it was true. Then she mentioned how she was a third-degree black belt. That hit me like a ton of bricks. We teach people to physically defend themselves, but what about the emotional abusers? Our teaching in this area was severely lacking. I believe, if other martial art instructors will admit it, they are lacking in this area as well.

That was the inspiration for this book. I wrote a book on the subject titled *Positive Defensive Behavior*. We self-published the book, so we were unable to get it into the brick-and-mortar bookstores. But it was good practice for this book, *Martial Hearts*, which you are about to read. I truly hope it inspires you and your family.

Introduction

Ready, Fire, Aim

HAVE YOU EVER asked a young person, "Why did you do that?" or perhaps "What were you thinking?" and they answered, "I don't know."?

Research from *The Medical Institute* shows they actually, in fact, *don't* know. Rather than think something through, young people form a thought, act upon that thought, and later reason it through (if they reason it at all).

This is a major reason why youth need proper guidance as they mature into adulthood. In fact, the human brain develops into full physical size around the age of twelve. However, it takes much longer (up to age twenty-five) to reach adult thinking. This is when the cognitive processing has fully developed in the prefrontal cortex.

Some components of cognitive processing (or thought) are emotional reasoning, critical thinking, planning, judgment, impulse control, and reactionary behavior.

To use a very basic word picture of how the brain develops cognitively, there are times when the brain's wiring trims, prunes, and reroutes used and unused processing functions to develop the input of social environment, defensive situations, personal interactions, etc. It is, therefore, our duty to help children learn proper development of their decision making through positive guidance and role modeling, to help them learn to make decisions for themselves.

Those who enroll into most martial arts programs have pumped up the fight-or-flight instinct with skilled defensive reactions. Our target response for this book is to incorporate that same physical defensive reflex with an emotionally defensive response. A *defensive mental edge* against those who would use con games, intimidation, or other forms of mental abuse against us, our friends, and loved ones. This is explained in more detail in the following.

What is a defensive mental edge? It is the ability to recognize the tactics of a potential emotional abuser. This emotional preparedness will afford you a decisive and speedy response to personal psychological threats. It ranges from the con of a casual acquaintance to a potentially abusive dating relationship.

Whether the nature of attack is physical or psychological, self-defense is more than a protective skill. It is a way of life. When we teach children to look both ways before crossing the street or to beware of strangers, we are teaching them defensive behavioral skills. But it actually begins even earlier.

Think about this for a moment. We all know nutrition and exercise have direct bearing on a healthy body.

The whole child concept of teaching includes the need for proper nutrition. Therefore, when we try to prevent an infant from spitting out his or her carrots, we are teaching a behavior to obtain proper nutrition, and so the concept of self-defense has begun. So what went wrong? We'll get to that, but first allow me to further explain the basis for this book.

The focus of this manual is to educate children, teens, and young adults using the whole child training concept. The whole child concept encompasses every aspect of adult preparedness from defensive awareness to defensive behavior. This would entail physical self-defense, academics, nutrition, exercise, respect, parental input, and emotional preparedness. Rather than focus on one area, such as drugs, alcohol, or premature sex, we focus on how to recognize the cons or bullies who would coerce or force a young person into such risky behaviors.

A young lady can have all the intention of saving herself as the most precious gift to give her future life partner, but if she is persuaded to get drunk at a party, she may end up pregnant and have no memory of the act. The true whole child concept would encourage right choices as well as physical self-defense training, which will give her the confidence and ability to stand up for her convictions. Youth with these skills are developing the defensive mental edge. Emotionally strong people have better chances of making quick, decisive decisions that can save their lives in more ways than the physical. This helps to instill a sense of self-worth. People who feel better about themselves make better choices. At one time, the thought was that youth just needed to have the discipline to say no. My experience has taught me that discipline without positive direction is just a habit. An alcoholic may not be able to keep a job, but he has the discipline to always find that next drink. *The choice of behavior must be the decision of the youth themselves.*

Review

What is a defensive mental edge?

1. The ability to recognize when someone is catching on to your game.
2. The ability to recognize the tactics of a potential emotional abuser.
3. The ability to recognize con games so you can turn the tables on them.
4. None of the above.

An example of a *potential* emotional abuser is:

1. Checks phone numbers and e-mail list.
2. Throws a fit if the toilet paper does not hang the right way.
3. Both 1 and 2.
4. None of the above.

What is the whole child concept?

1. It encompasses every aspect of physical and mental preparedness for adult life.
2. It encompasses every aspect of learning proper parenting skills for rearing a child.
3. Both 1 and 2.
4. None of the above.

Examples of the whole child concept include:

1. The physical and mental ability to stand by desired right choices.
2. Strict discipline and obedience.
3. Plenty of free time, chores, and homework.
4. All of the above.

A direct focus of the whole child concept is:

1. Always be prepared for safe sex should the urge become too great.
2. Recognize cons or bullies who would coerce or force a young person into risky behavior.
3. Recognize when situations are beginning to get out of hand at parties where drugs and alcohol are being used.
4. Recognize cons so you can turn the tables of them.

Review Answers

What is a defensive mental edge?

1. The ability to recognize when someone is catching on to your game.
2. **The ability to recognize the tactics of a potential emotional abuser.**
3. The ability to recognize con games so you can turn the tables on them.
4. None of the above.

An example of a *potential* emotional abuser is:

1. Checks phone numbers and e-mail list.
2. Throws a fit if the toilet paper does not hang the right way.
3. **Both 1 and 2.**
4. None of the above.

What is the whole child concept?

1. **It encompasses every aspect of physical and mental preparedness for adult life.**
2. It encompasses every aspect of learning proper parenting skills for rearing a child.
3. Both 1 and 2.
4. None of the above.

Examples of the whole child concept include:

1. **The physical and mental ability to stand by desired right choices.**
2. Strict discipline and obedience.
3. Plenty of free time, chores and homework.
4. All of the above.

A direct focus of the whole child concept is:

1. Always be prepared for safe sex should the urge become too great.
2. **Recognize cons or bullies who would coerce or force a young person into risky behavior.**
3. Recognize when situations are beginning to get out of hand at parties where drugs and alcohol are being used.
4. Recognize cons so you can turn the tables of them.

1
Life's Not a Hamburger, It's a Casserole

- ➢ Why is child obesity an American epidemic?
- ➢ Why is child depression on the rise?

THERE ARE MANY factors why these are happening. Trying not to be judgmental, one factor may be the significant number of today's parents who allow their children to make all of the decisions for their lifestyle and activities. Children need to start learning how to make choices for themselves in some areas, such as sports, but not in every area, such as switching sports every two to four weeks. *Just because we live in a more technologically advanced society today doesn't mean that children have developed a more advanced cognitive thought and no longer have the desire for immediate gratification.* They need parental *guidance* beyond "don't do what I do."

If we really want our children to grow up healthy, we need to make the sacrifices required to set good examples for them. It's alarming to see families pour out of a van, and it's the overweight eight-year-old, the overweight twelve-year-old, and the grossly overweight mom, aunt, and grandma. Please don't think I'm being critical. I'm just pointing out the truth concerning the growth of our nation. Children born into the overweight society are going to start having heart attacks at fourteen. That's not a laughing matter. It is, however, a depressing daily lifestyle for many young people.

It's also overwhelming to think "what do I do, how do I help myself?" It's not a diet that is needed; it's a life change in eating habits. You must learn to eat smaller portions. Eat what you want, but eat in moderation. If that's too hard to do, try this: don't buy that bag of chips. Just snack on grapes. That's it for now. Also, if you spend much time on the computer, get up and walk around about every thirty minutes. The same for watching television: get up and walk around during the commercials. Make your kids get up and walk around with you. Walk to the mailbox; later to the corner of the street. Eventually, you can make it around the block. After this, you won't need the riding shopping basket at the local grocery store. It's simple; it's just not easy.

I told you the total child concept had to come from the home as well as the school. It would also help if coaches stopped allowing the jocks to pick on the underdeveloped. The jocks should be encouraging other children to progress.

You can see how this is going to take a lot of effort and a lot of time, hence the chapter title. A hamburger you can buy or throw together in a matter of minutes, but a casserole takes time to prepare and tend and nurse until it is ready. But what a great dish. It is worth it just to hear people rave on how good it is. Life is like that. You can take the quick way of the sloppy, unhealthy life, or you can use this book to prepare our kids for a healthy adulthood. It's difficult, time-consuming, and requires much long-suffering. But, in the end, it is worth every painful day of sacrifice.

Without condemnation, here is a list of some modern family unit situations:

1. Biological and blended families who eat supper together (without iPods or cell phones), play board games on Saturday night, vacation with one another, and spend other quality time together. By the way, quality time is doing something with our kids. It's not driving them from activity to activity.
2. Single-parent families who are just trying to survive without help from an ex, the government, or the church.
3. Divorced and blended families where one or both parents attempt to influ-

> "...his tantrums have disappeared within two months"
>
> Cecil and Kim O
> GPs of five-year-old

ence their child to believe and act contrary to the other parent's teachings.
4. Families where the parents just don't want to accept responsibility for making decisions, or they don't want to put up with the whining they are forced to endure, since they don't believe in disciplining the child. They may even just be more concerned with trying to prevent their own marriage (or their life) from falling apart.

To now, it appears that marriage is so difficult, why try? Why not just live together? Well, that's the bottom line in today's concept of marriage, living together, or just hooking up. It is the illusion that sex, in itself, is a relationship. Well, it's not.

Well-meaning organizations came together traveling into the inner cities, where negative statistics on crime, poverty, and teen pregnancy were worse than any other demography. Their message was to save sex for marriage. Unknown to these well-meaning organizations, the inner city kids did not understand the concept of marriage. Their parents weren't married, and no one they knew had married parents.

Then opposing organizations would come in and say the first group says the answer is to never have sex, ever! Then, for some reason, one of the save sex speakers began comparing those who have had premarital sex to worn out shoes or chewed gum. In my experience, both organizations are wrong!

Whether you made the decision to have sex or you were forced, you are not worn out shoes or chewed gum. I look at it like this: You find a one-hundred-dollar bill on the ground. It's torn, scuffed, and dirty. What's the value on that piece of paper? One hundred dollars! It has value, the value you assign to it. My marriage license was important to me because my marriage was important to me. My high school diploma was important to me for the same reason. Then I worked hard to learn the skill of writing, and I use that skill to try and help others to understand life's lessons, such as attaching value to things that are important to others, like you are important. You are! But values must have a standard. America's standard of value originally came from God. Now don't get nervous. I will not preach at you. This is just instructive information based on defensive thinking, and I would be amiss not to point out this proven source of training in values, discipline, and appropriate social behavior.

Many relationships break up due to a lack of the basic moral obedience to God's standard of values. This obedience is one that requires loyalty and honor and sacrifice. It's not done on purpose, they just don't know anything about God or His values. We've grown up in a social system that took prayer out of schools and replaced it

> *"We have seen his self-confidence grow, his rebelliousness shrink (how many parents of thirteen-year-olds can say that), and his interest in and empathy toward others increase tremendously."*
>
> John and Judith D.
> Parents of teenager

with the concept of "whatever you feel is right, is right for you." This grew into the attitude of it's-all-about-me. Recognizing the selfishness growing in the country, the advertisers were quick to jump on it. "Have it your way" was a popular slogan. There was one ad, which was so bold, and it stated that life was all about appearance. The next scene had to happen.

People became arrogant: "It's all about me." Then they would hook up with someone else, believing the same life-is-all-about-me attitude. Then the babies started coming, and they let you know quickly when they wanted something. I saw one house full of stuffed animals because mom and dad *had* to buy their little one something to calm her down each and every time they went shopping. How can two people successfully live together and raise children while they're making separate decisions based on separate wants, and then have a child who demands even more differences? So what do we do? Start by finishing this book and refer to it often. Maybe you don't need everything in it, but I promise you'll learn enough to not only help yourself, but to help others who want to receive the peace you have found.

So what does all this mean? It means whatever's worth having is worth culturing and developing slowly on the basis of merit, as opposed to pie-in-the-sky promises. Further investigation in this book will reveal techniques which, if practiced, will reward you with the successful long-lasting relationship we all crave. If sex is something that drives your life, following the examples and suggestions in this book regarding developing healthy relationships will grant you the best sexual pleasure for which you could ever wish. But remember, it's not a meet-and-defeat relationship. It takes time to simmer and develop into deeply satisfying nourishment for your soul. Life is not a hamburger from a fast-food relationship, it's a carefully prepared casserole from a slowly developed love. A love that craves marriage as a way to show your partner that you want only to be with her forever. That's love!

2

Who's in Charge Here?

Section 1: Children

Young children, preschool through elementary age, should be learning to make right choices while still learning obedience to the parent(s) or guardians. This will help them in young adulthood to still rely on their parents or other trusted adults for guidance on issues they don't yet quite understand.

Nothing has been as destructive to the people of our country as the detriment of the family unit. But rather than seek blame, we need to look for answers that deal with the reality of where we are today in the family household. This information is presented without pity or apology. It is a simple, although difficult, set of tools for those who wish to move forward for the benefit of future generations to grow and develop into successful family units of their own.

The most catastrophic situation is in divorced or single-parent families, so we will begin there. Do not skip this part, even if your family has no need of it, or if it is terribly difficult to bear. Your knowledge of it may benefit others.

Separated parents should support morally sound boundaries set by the custodial parent. For example: "Mom doesn't allow us to watch R-rated movies at home. But we get to at dad's house. There is more freedom at dad's house. He loves us more." Sometimes it's just plain common sense decisions, such as never making the children brush their teeth or bathe when one parent has custody, using the child to hurt the other parent.

> "...(he) has been able to discontinue all medication and counseling."
>
> Lynn S.
> Mother of a
> seven-year-old

These behaviors could be part of today's practice of allowing the child to make decisions for the family, when it should be the other way around. The best way to take back control of the child is by letting them have choices. At dinner, for example—"Would you like to have milk or water?"—you offer them the choices, but they feel empowered because they made a choice regarding their meal. Try it.

Let's say a child wants to become involved in a sport. Make a list of sports available in your area and ask the child to choose one (and only one). Have him agree to participate regularly for a specific length of time. Start small, maybe six weeks. You may even wish to make a written contract between you and the child to help them learn what many of us adults learned the hard way. Don't let them quit the chosen sport because it's too hard, or they have to practice, or they sweat. They may just sit on the bench, but they are going to be there until the agreed time is over. On the other hand, as their protector, do not force them to stay if the mentor is abusive or a negative-role model.

Remember also that the sport is for the child. Many a father has ruined his son's knees, forcing him to participate in a sport that the father thought would someday bring million-dollar paychecks to the family.

When the agreed time has passed, praise the child for their commitment, and ask them if they'd like to continue in their elected endeavor or choose a different sport or other activity (not video games or television). If we guide and support our children, they will have a much better chance of finding an activity they really enjoy. But no break from physical fitness programs!

> "Mr. Passmore makes me feel like a winner."
>
> Katie L.
> Preteen

Children begin forming their character very early in life. Too often children are treated as unintelligent nuisances rather than blessings. Why is it that we may spend more time watering and caring for our lawn and flowers than we will spend nurturing our children? Could it be because it's all about me (and my image)?

The parent of a very young child asked me after her daughter's first self-defense class how I was able to hold her daughter's attention for an entire hour. "She never listens to me," said the mom. "Well," I answered, "how often do you listen to her?" In this particular case, as the class began, the child started to tell me something. I listened intently for a few seconds and then told her it was karate time, and I would very much like to hear her story after class. She was quiet and focused for the duration of the fifty-minute class.

Listen as if the silly things they say are the most important things in the world. Stopping to look at them occasionally as you listen is very important. When instructing the child, be sure your child feels engaged in a conversation and not just stuck with another lecture. And look at them. Don't you make them look at you when you are talking to them? We are always setting examples that the kids will mimic.

Parenting classes provide awesome tips for accomplishing desired performance from our children. This helped me to be a better martial arts trainer, and I recommend parenting classes for parents and grandparents, but I also recommend it to any professional who works with children. Jot down some local parenting class information (you may try a local church or two).

Section 2: Youth

Junior-high-age youth are making the transition into mature, adult thinking. Work *with* them to enforce healthy choices. Remember, give them options and allow them to choose. They also need to know that you have their back if they stand firm in doing the right thing. For example: you have a daughter who tells you she is receiving peer pressure to dress more provocatively. How do you respond? Do you tell her it's okay? Or do you tell her how proud you are of her modesty and encourage her to be her own person? Although a healthy social life is important at any age, those in school need to remember they are preparing for life in adulthood (they're not already in it). That being said, how do you, as an adult, behave and dress as role model for youth?

> *"The program developed his character through gentle mentoring."*
>
> Allan S., parent

The most provocative bathing suit I saw last year was worn by a mother of two small children.

If our kids come to us, and we reject them by dismissing their concerns, they may stop coming to us for advice. It's serious to them. We must be a positive role model for them (you'd be surprised how attentive they are when you think they are *not* listening).

A very beautiful young teen came to me because, regardless of her modest behavior, the boys treated her like a whore. I told her it was probably the provocative clothes she wore. Her response was, "What? I dress like my mom." Then there is the other side of the coin. Men who take teens to *Hooters* because they like the wings is the same lie as men who buy *Playboy* magazines because they like to read the articles.

Section 3: Pre-Adults

High-school-age young people are cementing the character that will guide their adult lives. We need to encourage them to think for themselves and not echo the opinions of the media, their friends, or even us. We must allow them to form their own opinions, even when we disagree, and we must reinforce the boundaries set by school rules, social etiquette, and civil law until they are grown and out on their own. They will still need some advice from time to time in their early adult life. We can only be there for them, but we *must* be there for them, even after they marry.

Statistics have shown that married men perform better and earn more money than unmarried men, and that married mothers are half as likely to be victims of domestic violence. Reports also show that 80 percent of all children in never-married families suffer long-term poverty. To prevent this from happening to you, you should practice the skills learned in this book until it is a habit.

3

Demons from the Id

WE ALL FACE challenges in life. Some of us face these challenges every day. No amount of comforting can overcome these tormenting demons. Kids who are bullied develop physical problems; such as, loss of appetite, stomach aches, diminishing grades, bad behavior, etc. Also, the bullied often become bullies themselves. "Not MY child." You say. Of course. The denial of these types of problems will delay seeking help for the child. Here appears a demon created from our very own minds to deny or compensate for this problem. But there is this and so many other things which we CAN overcome with acceptance, knowledge, courage and sacrifice.

> *"...since our last meeting, she has improved in all areas at school! She is definitely much happier, and her schoolwork shows it. Thank you for taking action so quickly."*
>
> Jennifer D.
> School Teacher

Whatever the cause of our demons, we must first identify the problem within ourselves before we can confront others (if it is a problem, such as bullying). But what about the anger and frustration we cause ourselves? For example: you sign up for a scuba excursion while on a cruise. At the beach preparing for the dive, the group leader (wanting to make a little more money) tells everyone to rent a locker to stow their gear. You didn't bring any money because your travel buddy said he was bringing a few dollars. Unknown to you, he spent it all in the little marketplace the tour visited before coming to the beach. The fear of having all of your personal effects stolen begins to burn, turning from fear to anger. You lash out at your friend, blaming him for spending his money. "I just won't go," you say. Now you are on the way toward rage.

Your friend calmly asks the scuba group leader what to do since you have no money. "No problem," he answers. "You can just leave it in the office." Now you can calm down and enjoy the underwater delights. Before we can identify the wrong thinking of others, we must first be able to identify the wrong thinking within ourselves. The next page identifies several different types of thought, which can get us in trouble when there may have been a much simpler way of dealing with the demon.

It works best if you look for these in yourself rather than someone else. However, once you have done so, you may see them happening in others. Knowing this can help you understand what's going on with them and prevent your lashing out at them in defense. You may then find a way to solve the problem without letting it ruin your day. In other words, get your own house in order before judging others.

4
Types of Thought

ALL-OR-NOTHING THINKING. LOOKING at things in absolute, extreme, black-and-white categories. For example: "It's either my way or the highway."

Overgeneralization. Viewing one negative event as a never-ending pattern of defeat. For example: "I have a criminal record, I'll never get a job."

Mental filter. Dwelling on the negative; filtering out and ignoring the positive. For example: You perform outstanding in ten areas and poorly in one. Putting all of your focus on the one poor performance and staying depressed over it is dwelling on the negative.

Discounting the positives. Insisting that your successes don't count. For example: "Staying sober for one weekend is no big deal if I'm trying to quit drinking forever."

Jumping to conclusions. **Mind reading**. Assuming that people are reacting negatively without evidence. For example: "He doesn't like me because he's white."

Jumping to conclusions. **Fortune-telling**: Predicting bad outcomes without evidence. For example: "He won't hire me because I've been in prison."

Magnifying/Minimizing. Magnifying, overreacting. For example: "What you said ruined my entire life." Minimizing, ignoring important things. For example: "One blunt won't hurt." (Note: a *blunt* is a fairly new term for a marijuana joint.)

Emotional Reasoning. Accepting feelings as facts. For example: "I feel stupid, therefore, I am stupid."

Should statements. Criticizing self/others with shoulds, oughts, musts. For example: "You shouldn't feel that way."

Labeling. Putting negative labels on self/others rather than labeling the action. For example: "I'm a failure," rather than saying, "I failed a test today."

Personalization and blame. Blaming oneself unfairly, or unfairly blaming others. For example: "My wife made me hit her by not having my supper ready before the game."

Working Through Types of Thoughts

Situation: What happened?

Michael interrupted me in the middle of my story with something he did that was much better.

What were you thinking just before and during the unpleasant feeling?

Happiness interrupted by the feeling of being upstaged.

Emotions, feelings:

I felt wounded, like he stole my joy so he could dominate the room.

More accurate or more helpful thoughts:

I could have said "that's great Michael. Why don't you tell us about that when I've finished sharing my story?"

Action taken to overcome feeling:

Went for a walk in the park, enjoying God's creation until the joyful feeling returned.

Other action one could do to feel better:

Talk with someone in worse condition than myself.

"I especially like how you teach that courtesy is the first line of self-defense."

Betty N.
Parent

See if you can add a situation and follow it through with the steps above.

_____

_____

_____

_____

_____

_____

_____

_____

Many of the following chapters make good training sessions for youth. However, there is material that college students have found extremely helpful as well.

5

Planning Your Future

A Study Guide for Young People of Any Age

IN APPROXIMATELY TEN to fifteen years from right now, *you* may be running this country. Now that you have been made aware of this, what do you want to be doing ten years from now? What is the picture of your own happy adult life? What are your dreams? Do you see yourself as one of the following (or something similar)?

- Professional athlete
- Doctor or Astronaut

A young man I met is a very talented artist now serving a thirty-year prison sentence for armed robbery so he could buy twenty-dollars worth of drugs. This was not his plan for the future. This could easily be any of us who delve into drugs. Think about what you want to do today to reach your dreams of tomorrow.

- School teacher
- Movie star
- Millionaire
- Mom or Dad
- Policeman or fireman
- Military Sergeant, General, or Admiral
- President or Scientist

It's good to have dreams. All of the adults with positions listed above were young people just like you who made their dreams become reality. So what would be any obstacles that could prevent you from doing the same thing?

Money, or not having it, is a big problem for many young people in going to college. But there are organizations that are willing to pay your college expenses provided you stay off drugs and have good grades. Remember how we stated earlier that *you* may be running the country within the next ten to fifteen years? Well, we (the senior citizens) want to support you so you can make good community leaders. Our time will be over, and we will be passing the responsibility of leadership on to you. Therefore, it is in our best interests to see you become successful in achieving your dreams. And we don't care about your skin

> *"They become successful in different areas and can manage stress in difficult situations."*
>
> Richard D.
> College Language Specialist
> for the Deaf

color, religion, sex, nationality, or faith. First, however, you must finish high school successfully. Then you may set your sights on a college career and the job of your choice. We want *you* to succeed. You may think you will just drop out of school and get rich selling drugs. Remember the young man in prison. Wrong behavior (or sin) will take you farther than you want to go.

Have you ever thought about school as your job? Think about it. Most adults go to an eight-to-five job. Sometimes work will pile up, and they need to work late to get caught up. We call that overtime, for which most people receive overtime pay.

You basically do the same thing, except you get out earlier. Right? Wrong. You still need to go home to review and prepare for the next day's new skills. You work on this homework until quitting time at five o'clock. If you don't finish, then you need to put in some overtime. Whereas adults are paid with money, students are paid with knowledge. College is attended for specialized knowledge which, in return, grants higher-paying, more prestigious jobs. You may even contribute to making a better world. There may be a young person out there right now who will someday find a cure for cancer. That is, if you are able to finish high school with a drug-free education. Finish high enough in your grades, and the college as well as other programs may pay *all* of your tuition.

Now, if no tragedy (such as war, illness, etc.) occurred, and money was no object, is there anything *you* might do, which would stop your dreams from coming true? It's a safe bet to say you probably would like a career that requires a few years of dedicated study. But I'm sure your dream is not to be in prison for drugs, sexual abuse, neglecting your children, or for beating a family member to death in a fit of rage. Yet our prisons are full of men and women who, as youth, wanted to be doctors and scientists and famous athletes. We live in a society that focuses on what you want at this very moment. The hamburger, and not the casserole. It's often difficult to see your daily life as part of achieving a desired future. However, what you are doing today is affecting your future.

Do kids attend early-morning football or band practice because they enjoy getting up before the sun? Do they practice for another one or two hours after school because they don't want to go home and relax? No! They do it because they want to perform well at the Friday night game. The daily sacrifice of hard work is worth the goal they have in mind. But even if the football team loses, or the band doesn't place at regionals, they will both be out there bright and early on Monday morning running those drills and playing those scales all over again.

> *"He sets their minds to establish the right attitude and confidence to succeed."*
>
> Toni G.
> School Teacher

When you return to school after the summer or to work after vacation, you always want to share what you did during the time off. Some may go to the beach. Others may go to a theme park. But you rarely (if ever) share about what it took to get there. When you share what you did in Europe, it normally doesn't even include the fourteen-hour plane ride in a small seat next to some large snoring stranger, or the fourteen-hour trip back sitting in front of a lady with a crying toddler. That's because it's the actual destination we strive for, and we forget what it takes to get there. It's the same with reaching the goals in your life. Every day is part of the journey to reach your desired goal, whether it's to be a doctor or a professional athlete.

Now what do you see, based on the activities of your daily life? What could stop you from reaching your desired profession ten or fifteen years from now? Your world just became much larger, didn't it? You never thought of it this way before, right?

If you're spending your day ignoring your study assignments and not caring about that test coming up, then you are already choosing to fail in life. So don't blame it on those mean old rich white men thinking they don't want you to succeed in life. I've already told you there are people and organizations who want to help you succeed in life so you can successfully run the country and even the world as an adult. And, guess what, many of those groups were founded by old rich white men.

It's too easy to just quit. But if you want that dream life to come true, don't start using drugs, drinking, skipping school, and spending hours a day in front of a television, or playing video games, or having sex. Yes, I said sex. We will get into the importance of this later. I know you want to look cool, but everyone else isn't wanting to reach your goals in life. There are many youth who want to play pro ball, but only a few make it. Why is that? Think about it. What are you doing today that would interfere with your body's peak performance later on?

Do you want to be a great doctor? Do you want to be the one who will discover the cure for cancer? Then what are you doing today, right now to prepare yourself for that future? You can't be killing your much-needed brain cells, rather than building them and rearranging them to learn and perform quickly and correctly. You can't be one of the hundreds of thousands of young people worrying if they are going to become pregnant, or where their lover is on Friday night, rather than worrying about that test on Monday. You get my meaning? I don't need to browbeat that into you. The choice is yours, so don't go blaming it on someone else.

Even if you have been doing all that, and even if your grades are terrible, you can start over right now. Work hard! You are doing this for *you*! You are the one who will benefit from it. But be prepared. Those people you thought were your friends, they may want you to fail. They know you're trying to improve your situation, and they don't want you to succeed. Watch. You'll see. Who are your friends? Your good time party friends, or those mean old rich white men you keep hearing about on the street or in the news? The news is not always a reliable source of accurate information. Try to believe nothing that you hear and only half of what you see.

This next chapter deals with tips and tricks to help you have more free time and better grades at school. You can waste time trying to look cool, or you can be cool for real. Learning how to organize is a very valuable asset in life.

Organizing Your Backpack and Locker

What does your room look like? Your backpack? Your locker? The bell rings. Oh no! My pencil is dull, and my pen is out of ink. The teacher announces, "Turn in your homework and copy notes from the board." She doesn't tolerate getting out of your seat to get supplies after the tardy bell rings.

You're thinking, *My homework! I can't remember where it is.* You start digging through your backpack. All that stuff, and you can't find another pencil or pen; even worse, you can't find your homework. You remember doing it at the coffee table while watching TV last night.

You can see the notes from today's first three classes. They're smashed on top of your books. Under those notes are the books for last period, this period, and next period. You pull the books out and dig around the bottom of your backpack. There are all kinds of papers squashed in the bottom of it.

None of them is the assignment you need. You start flipping through the books, just as the teacher rings the bell to indicate your notes should be finished and your assignment should be turned in. She'll be discussing the content of your notes and your homework. You hope she doesn't notice you.

You start leafing through the books. Finally, there (where the questions were in the book) is your homework. You smooth it out, scribble your name on it, and saunter over to the place where assignments are turned in. She notices—*busted*.

This section is designed to help you (or a friend who needs it) organize and coordinate in order to have more free time for play and/or socializing. This information may be helpful to kids, teens, and adults.

Organizing at Home

Find a place for everything school-related and keep it all in that area. Start with your home study spot. Where is it, and what does it look like? It needs to be in a quiet, yet well-lit, place in your home. Find a place away from distractions with all the supplies you need for your work: paper, pencil, pen, math tools, dictionary, thesaurus, and materials you will need for projects in progress.

If you don't like complete quiet, add some soothing music (preferably instrumental) on a soft volume. Good brain music would be classical, most are movie themes, or oldies. You don't want to end up dancing around the room when your concentration should be on academic study.

Use a homework folder and an assignment notebook. Get a two-pocket folder, no brads needed. On the left side, write "work to be finished." On the right side, write "work to turn in." If you do not finish work in class, put it in the left side of the folder. After you have finished work to be turned in on the next day, put it in the right side of the folder.

> *"He can complete most of his work in class and very little work does he take home."*
>
> Zac P.
> Parent

The assignment notebook can be a spiral, used only for this particular purpose. The spiral can be regular-sized or as small as a three-fifth spiral. The important thing to remember is to only use it for writing your assignments. Ripped-out spiral paper is a bit messy. Neat papers make a better impression than smoothed-out papers found squashed in the bottom of your backpack after it should have already been turned in. Your teachers now believe you are giving your best.

When you get home, put your books in the same place until you are ready to do your homework. When you finish, pack everything neatly into your backpack, and set it near the door or some other spot every day. Always use the same spot where you can pick it up on your way out the door for school. That's called a "drop spot."

Doesn't that sound easier? Waiting until the last minute to gather everything up never helps your day. Everyone in the household becomes frazzled before the day even begins if you're frantic about finding that one last thing every day.

Organizing at School

Let's talk about the backpack. Clean it out. It's not your trash can. Take the time to throw trash away as you go. If your teacher requests that you not get up in the middle of class to throw away trash, set it aside to throw away as you leave class.

More students are carrying backpacks to class now than ever before. If your teachers don't expect you to have a binder, try using spirals and folders. The best backpack I have seen has a spiral and a folder for each class. The spirals are for notes. The folders have loose-leaf paper in one pocket and assignments in the other. No trash!

Pockets in the backpack can be used to put pencils, pens, and other needed supplies, such as cell phones in case of an *emergency only*. Should cell phones and iPods even need to be at school? Does your *need* to have them outweigh the distraction?

Take time to find a good backpack. Place larger, heavier books closer to your back for proper balance. More and more injuries are being caused by backpacks. Swinging it off your arm without looking can hit someone. Leaving it out in the aisle in class can cause someone to trip over it. The backpack should be worn to and from school with *both* straps and not hanging down low over the small of your back. This strains

> *"I learned how to manage time and solve conflicts."*
>
> Melanie L.
> College Student

the muscles in the back and can cause serious injury. Don't risk football or other sports injuries due to strained back muscles just so you can look cool.

Now to the locker. Are you late to class because you spend too much time at your locker looking for what you need for your next class? Clean it out and organize it. A locker shelf is a good investment. If you don't like carrying a backpack, use the space under the shelf for folders, binders, and spirals. On the shelf, place your covered books in order of classes with the name of each class written on the spine.

As you pull out one book, put the last book on the right of the line of books. At the end of the day, check your assignment book to see which books need to be taken home for homework. Also, place in order your folder, binders, and spirals.

Our society moves at a fast pace. Organization will help you relax and feel better about school. You can become a more confident student when you follow the steps given in this chapter. The time you save with a little organization will give you more time for socializing with your friends. Your grades will improve, and you'll become more popular with a little free time. If bullies are a problem, get yourself down to the local martial arts school and start training on how to respond to physical aggression. Just be careful that you don't become a bully yourself.

Okay, let's review.

- Study in a place with as few distractions as possible and the materials you need for homework. Possible locations:

  _____

- Have a "drop spot" at home. Possible locations:

  _____

- Use a homework folder and assignment notebook.
  - homework folder bought
  - assignment notebook bought
- Your backpack is not your trash can. Clean it out and place everything in the order it is needed during the school day.
- Organize your locker with books placed in the order you will use them during the day.
- Your teachers will notice your organization.
- When you are organized, you have more free time for socializing with friends.

So now that you've mastered organizing, how good are you at studying? Don't freak out, there are many really smart people who could use better study habits. Let's go to the next part of this chapter and work on how we can have a more productive study time at home and at school.

Study Skills

Do you feel so overwhelmed that you just quit studying for tests? Do you think you waste studying all those hours only to make a fifty on that test? Does the information get stuck in your brain when the test hits your desk?

I knew of a lady who was forty years old before someone taught her how to study for a test. She had spent nineteen years in school as a borderline C student. Tests were her biggest problem, especially when trying to recall facts.

When she tried to go back to college and receive a degree, she was only able to take an introductory class. However, she learned some great ways to study. Here are some of the more simple techniques and a mention of some lengthy ones.

> *"It's a Miracle!"*
> Vicki A.
> Mother of teens

The brain is like a filing cabinet. Everyone has their own filing system. Some people simply open the drawer holding the desired information and pull it out. Some people know which drawer the information is in, but they must locate the specific folder desired. There are others who have difficulty finding the drawer and the folder holding the information.

What do the latter do? Some give up for lack of success on tests. Others learn how to mark the drawer and folder, making it

> *"It has taught me to have confidence in myself and to expect the best from myself."*
> Tiffany W.
> Ninth Grade,
> Alternative School

easier to find the information. My suggestions are for those who want to find the drawer and the folder when they get to the test.

Those who have given up will find hope in some of these suggestions, but it may not be much easier unless you practice using creativity. Individual creativity is necessary for success. This will take time, but you will find the results to be amazing.

Be active

The first trick is to be an avid listener. Take notes in class and also while you read textbooks. You will remember more if you write it down rather than just listen. Some teachers make note guides for lectures. Keep up with the teacher as she lectures and discusses. Jot down what you hear during discussions. It might help you remember an important fact. Naturally, you can't write down every word, but (with practice) you will find your own form of note-taking that works for you.

Trick number two is to be an active reader. Before you read an assignment, look through the passage. Read title, subtitles, and picture captions. If vocabulary is highlighted in your text, look the words up and learn what they mean. Even if you think you know what a word means, looking it up may give you a better understanding of words you only thought you knew really well. Next, read the passage. The sooner you learn this habit, the sooner your comprehension and memorization will increase. When you get into more complicated texts and have this habit already formed, you will find studying to be easier than you have experienced it in the past.

Fold a piece of paper lengthwise. Write questions that come to mind on the left side of the paper. Read or skim through the passage again to find the answers to your questions. Write the answers on the right side of the paper. If you have been given an assignment related to the text materials, now is the best time to answer the questions. It will be easier to find the correct answers since you are familiar with what is in the reading assignment. Many times, the answer is going to be obvious when you search for key words in the question.

> "...he now has '100' on all of his tests at school."
>
> Zac P.
> Parent

The third trick is note cards. Note cards are a great tool to use when memorizing information for a test. One lecturer told an interesting story: When he was in college, he would spend hours studying for tests. His buddies made cheat notes. He would make Cs on his tests; they would make As. He thought, *This guy is kind of dim. Of course they made As. They used their cheat notes.* Guess what? They didn't use their cheat notes. What happened? The cheat notes were active learning. He had studied passively. But this experience taught him the benefit of studying actively.

Use four by six index cards. On one side, write the question or vocabulary word you need to know. On the opposite side of the card, write the answer. If the answer is long, highlight key words to memorize. These words will help you remember the entire answer.

There are tips, often called hooks, to help you remember information. In your brain is information you already know (hooks). When you use stored information to hook to new information, it is easier to recall the new information. The hooks could be pictures or silly words. Include these on your note cards to recall facts.

Another trick is organizing lists to memorize. Logical ways to organize include alphabetical order, numerical order, using alliteration (the beginning sounds are the same), or using an acrostic (the first letters of the word or phrase spell another word).

These tricks leave you with less to recall and something on which to hook the new information for better results. Finally, lengthy answers can be broken down into phrases and then memorized. Practice this now on the lines below.

Write a short phrase or word you need to know. Then across the page from that, write your hook.

_____
_____
_____
_____
_____
_____

When You Get the Test

Read through the questions and answer the ones you confidently know. The ones you are less sure of can be answered with memory tricks.

True/False questions can be tricky. Some teachers like to make them sound true. Some teachers will state the obvious or not-so-obvious. If a word in question reminds you of one used in studying, draw the picture. Write on your test whatever you need to write or draw to help you answer correctly. If you are still stumped, go on to the rest of the test. Something else on the test may remind you of earlier answers.

Multiple choice questions contain answers that can be eliminated before choosing the correct answer. You can eliminate definitely incorrect answers and then choose the most correct answer. When you know an answer is incorrect, draw a single line through it. Only use one line to write through the incorrect answer. This helps your brain know what is left. Next, read the choices left using any memory tricks you used in studying to help you find the correct answer.

Matching questions can be answered in much the same way. Answer questions you definitely know, then use memory tricks to answer the rest. Check through when you're finished for choices you may have used twice. When asked to write a list, first write your memory trick for that question. Then write in the answer.

Don't waste time lingering over a question stumping you before you have answered as many questions as you can in a shorter amount of time. Sometimes the brain freezes as you get frustrated over one question early in the test. You will become more likely to miss more questions as your frustration increases over missed questions. Put the pencil down and take four or five deep breaths (you will learn relaxation breathing in a later chapter). Then continue with the test.

As you move on through the test, an earlier answer may come to mind. If you feel yourself getting anxious, a couple more breaths to relax. Then go back to your test. Tell yourself you can do it. When you make a higher grade, celebrate!

Waiting until the last minute to cram is a sure journey to failure. You are only putting information into short-term memory. Remember, your goal isn't just to make As. Your goal is to learn, building upon that with more knowledge, which you will use in your adult life. As you learn, the As will come.

Handling Long Study Sessions

If you know you are going to be studying for a long time, plan ahead. The best thing you can do as soon as you get home is relax and eat a snack. Play outside for about thirty minutes. This will help you work out some of the stress you feel from sitting in classes all day. Forget the television and video games. They only put your brain to sleep and don't relax you.

Get the hard studying out of the way first. Start with your least favorite or hardest subject. Study for about twenty minutes at a time. The V theory says the information in the first and last ten minutes at one session is what you will remember the best.

After twenty minutes, go get a drink, go to the restroom, play with your pet, or talk to your parents, siblings, or guardian. Give yourself about five minutes and go back for another twenty-minute session. When you have finished with a long study session, reward yourself with a phone call to a friend, visiting with a friend, watching a television show, playing a video game, or doing something you like doing.

> *"He can focus attention on the instructions his teacher is telling him. His attitude and behavior have both improved."*
>
> Zac P.
> Parent

The study time waltz

Studying, for an unorganized person, can be a chore. Getting and staying organized and planning ahead will bring success and will make school more interesting and fun. The more fun it becomes, the more you'll enjoy practicing it. The more you practice it, the better you get at it. The better you get at it, the more fun it becomes. I call that *the study time waltz*.

Remember that learning is your job. Just as adult jobs pay money, your job pays knowledge. Your knowledge, measured by grades, is what you will need to run the country and to make your dreams come true. Each year is a building block of knowledge, increasing your ability to achieve success in life. So the big question is, what are you willing to do *today* to make your dream a reality? Maybe a better question is: What are you willing to quit? Trying to be popular? Using alcohol and/or drugs? Manipulating people so you can have status? Or are you willing to focus on your life? The life you will have when your dream is coming true, and it will!

Things To Remember

- Take notes in class.
- Get to know the test assigned before answering questions.
- Write your own questions to be answered during the second reading.
- Answer questions the teacher has assigned.
- Make note cards to use when studying for tests.
- Use memory tricks to help you remember facts when taking a test.
- When taking the test, answer the questions you do know first, then use memory tricks to help you answer questions less familiar to you.
- Break long study sessions into twenty-minute segments.
- Reward yourself for a job well done.

Now that you have more time for socializing with your friends, you will find that you will have more opportunities to make new friends as well. Sometimes, we don't always hit it off with new people. The following personal interaction skills will help defuse a potentially physical confrontation before it escalates into a violent situation. The best self-defense is when an altercation doesn't happen at all.

Although this set of tools for defensive behavior are important, I recommend taking a martial arts class in order to give you the confidence to stand firm on your moral decisions. You have a plan for your future, as we found before, and you don't want anyone forcing or coercing you into wrong behavior. One more thing to remember about joining a martial arts school: don't get so caught up in the tournaments that you neglect your schoolwork. I've seen that done a lot. These classes are to help you with your education—not to become your new life.

I further recommend you encourage others in your martial arts class to get a copy of this book and use it to supplement their training. Being a black belt doesn't mean you can't marry someone who abuses you emotionally with tongue-fu. Although I joke, it really is a very serious situation, one you want to avoid. And boys (and men) can be emotionally abused, as well as girls (and women). Trust me, I know.

The one other thing which may be out of our control is bullying. Just as I had predicted more than twenty years ago, bullying has become a big problem. At that time, schools opposed martial arts training, assuming we taught violence. Now we have become more recognized for teaching peaceful methods of resolving conflict, leaving physical self-defense as a last resort. However, sometimes you get a bully who just wants to prey on those weaker than themselves. I have long thought people bully because they are insecure. It could be the preacher demanding control, the deacon's wife still trying to win prom queen, the career military person expecting their orders be carried out without question, or the kid down the street. Often, with children, they are jealous because you make good grades, or you're a happy person, or your family spends time with you. Whatever the reason, bullying is a method for insecure people to either get their way or to feel better about themselves.

In olden times, like the '60s and '70s, bullies would give you a bloody nose and then go about their business. In today's times, people are more cowardly and less respectful of human life. They will drive by your house and spray it with gunfire. Or they will attack your character on the Internet. Cyberbullying has become an entire issue of its own. Of course, most instructors teach to walk away whenever possible, "Sticks and stones may break my bones, but words will never harm me." That is what we were told as children. Well, that's no longer true. Words hurt people today very deeply.

We've changed society to be more apathetic toward others, but we've taken it to an extreme. Tournaments, for example, taught us to work as a team, and the losing built character.

Now everyone must be a winner so that no feelings get hurt. Then when today's youth (and even adults) are insulted on the Internet, they need counseling. Some poor, abused youth have even committed suicide over it. It's a heartbreaking situation for those of us who have spent a lifetime building young people up so they could cope with the problems of life. For me, it was using examples of a struggling relationship or marriage, not getting the job you wanted, or even losing your job. But I never imagined that people would be so devastated by slander on social media. It is a real problem that needs to be addressed.

The reason I believe so strongly in taking a martial arts class is because it teaches confidence. If a person develops confidence and discipline, it doesn't matter if they never find themselves in a physical altercation. They will have benefitted from the class emotionally. Which is exactly what *Martial Hearts* is about. Now let's learn some ways to interact positively with others in society.

6
Important Social Skills

Although the format of this section is for classroom instruction, there are places for those reading this book to practice individual activities. They may also practice group activities with friends or siblings for fun and to share this valuable information with others. They are great icebreakers at birthday parties and other gatherings.

1. Disagreeing
2. Accepting criticism
3. Compliment vs. Flattery
4. Asking for help
5. Expressing feelings appropriately
6. Following instructions
7. How to accept being told "NO!"
8. Expressing empathy and understanding
9. How to apologize

10. How to accept an apology
11. Greeting
12. How to answer and speak on the phone
13. Car courtesy
14. Walking courtesy
15. Dining courtesy
16. Indoors
17. Persons in conversation
18. School or business
19. Discourteous people

The following written format begins easier to understand for those who struggle with reading skills. It gradates, however, into more difficult word usage. Do not be discouraged. Have a dictionary available for definitions. Definitions are used in the beginning. Later on, you will need to look up definitions to increase your vocabulary. In fact, you can start right now by looking up the word *gradate* used earlier in this paragraph.

Disagreeing

Dis.a.gree (dĩs ə̄ –grē) v.i. pres. part. Dis-a-gree-ing past and past part. To differ in opinion or total ǁ to quarrel, squabble

Everyone disagrees. Learning to disagree appropriately instills

Lack of power is our dilemma.
Alcoholics Anonymous

tolerance and acceptance of others. Those who do not learn this important skill may be at a higher risk of violence than those who have strong communication skills. As adults, those without these skills may also be at a higher risk of developing uncontrollable rage, alcoholism, and other problems.

When someone disagrees with us, we can experience a sense of loss, such as loss of power or control. Persons without the ability to accept the different opinions of others and appropriately express their feelings may shut down completely or take control of the situation emotionally or physically, or both.

Through my experience as a professional self-defense instructor, I have learned that many adolescents, youth, and adults have experienced some form of altercation due to a lack of good communication skills.

Here is a basic outline to follow for an appropriate disagreement:

1. Look at the other person.
2. Use a pleasant voice.
3. Say "I understand you feel differently."
4. Tell why you feel differently.
5. Give a reason.
6. Listen to the other person.

Danny Passmore

Interactive activity

Divide into small groups and discuss opinions. Groups can be as small as two people or as large as six. It's really up to the teacher or activity leader on group sizes. Tell participants not to argue or be indifferent. Here are some suggested opinions to get the class started:

Are zebras white with black stripes or black with white stripes? This is not a debate where one side must win over the opposite side. It is an exercise in disagreeing without negative controversy. These are past compromises or agreements made in my class:

> Zebras are white with black stripes.
> Zebras are black with white stripes.
> Male zebras are one color, and females the other.
> Zebras are born white with brown stripes, which turn black with age.

Here are some other opinions that have been discussed in seminars:

1. The sky is full of white clouds. No blue sky can be seen behind the clouds. Is the sky white, or is the sky blue?
2. Can Spiderman beat up Superman?
3. Is it cold or is it warm in the room?
4. Does chocolate ice cream taste better than vanilla ice cream?

After a short amount of time, stop and discuss outcomes within each group. Often healthy and sometimes surprising agreements, compromises, or acceptance of differences have resulted.

Ask students to engage in conversation until they find something they disagree on in real life and then practice this skill. This is part of giving them responsibility in the learning process and encouraging creative thinking. Repeat the activity with an opinion suggested by a student. Encourage everyone for thinking and be careful not to criticize anyone's idea.

More and more in today's society, opinions are being stifled if they do not conform to what is deemed to be politically correct. Mention that you disagree with an opinion stated by President Obama, and you may find yourself labeled as a racist. You may even be in danger of losing your job. It's prudent to consider if a thought might be better kept to yourself rather than stir up a frenzy of intolerance and criticism.

Accepting Criticism

__Crit-i-cism__ (krĭtĭ-sĭzəm) n. a spoken or written judgment concerning some matter resting on opinion.

Criticism can be either negative or positive. Although people may sometimes criticize because they disagree with us, occasionally it could be a form of corrective criticism with the intent of helping us learn. Teachers and adults often try and help children understand right from wrong. Sometimes, however, it is perceived as harsh lecturing.

It can be very difficult to stand quietly and let someone criticize your beliefs or actions. However, it helps to listen to what the person is saying and think about what truth there may be in it. Knowing this may help us to present our opinion in a manner that receives less criticism. Then again, the other person may be the one who has judged incorrectly.

> There is a difference between criticism and ridicule.

> ***Rid-i-cule*** *(rĭdĭ-kyūl) n. contemptuous laughter.*
>
> ***Con-tempt*** *(kən-tĕmpt) n. an attitude to something which one despises as worthless, insignificant or vile ‖ total disregard.*
>
> ***Sar-casm*** *(sarkăzəm) n. a cruelly humorous statement or remark made with the intention of injuring the self-respect of the person to whom it is addressed, usually by drawing attention to one of his weaknesses and often associated with irony.*

We also need to remember that there is a difference between criticism and ridicule. Ridicule can be in the form of sarcasm and/or contempt. Even if someone makes fun of or treats our opinions as worthless or insignificant, this advice on how to accept criticism works equally well. They may, in fact, be trying to provoke you into losing your cool. Remember that others still need to respect your right of personal space.

Whether the person is giving criticism or ridiculing, here are some simple steps to follow:

1. Look at the person.
2. Say "okay."
3. Don't argue.

Interactive Activity

Have two actors practice for the class and get feedback. Demonstrate the wrong way that leads to hurt feelings or violence. Then, demonstrate the correct way to respond.

Female example.

Criticism: "Your face is as ugly as your shoes."

Unhealthy response: "Well, at least I match."

Healthy response: "I like my shoes. Your shoes are also very nice."

Allow youth to choose the criticism. It may be something they heard that very day.

Remember to interject use of space if the criticizing player begins to become loud and closes the distance (getting into the other player's face). (See "Boundaries.")

Next, have students suggest responses using correct social skills. You can do this as a class, individually, or as a homework assignment. Open discussion is very important for developing interpersonal skills. Encourage writing down suggestions as the students are reminded of them. Here is one of mine: I taught age three- and four-year-olds in thirty-minute classes with only six per class. Once I had to combine the classes so they were a little large. One boy, when the class was told to stand, told me "no." I told him to sit with his dad for a moment while I got the class in order. He quickly wanted to obey, but I made him sit with his dad for about thirty seconds and then invited him back into the class, and all was well. After the class, I received an angry phone call from the father. He believed I mishandled the situation (he was probably embarrassed) and announced to me the child is only three, and they will never be back to my school. I wanted to ask him at what age should a child start minding? Instead, I thanked him for letting me know and told him I would review my actions during the class to see if there was a better way I could have handled it. He stammered a little and then said, "Well, we aren't coming back." I told him I certainly understood and thanked him again for calling. Situation handled; no fight.

Now can you think of a situation, which you could have handled in a more positive way without being lured into an argument?

Compliments vs. Flattery

Com-pli-ment *(kŏmplə-mənt) n. a verbal expression of courteous praise ‖ an action showing praise and respect.*

Compliments are specific and sincere. Example: "I really admire how patient you are with your little brother." It is freely given with no strings attached in order to edify. A compliment could be as simple as telling someone they look nice. But if it becomes excessive (such as telling them they look nice every time you see them, or going on and on about how nice they look), then it could be flattery.

> ***Flat-ter-y*** *n. insincere or excessive praise.* ***To flatter includes****: in a calculating way.*

Flattery is insincere and misleading, with the intent of selfish gain. Example: "Oh, baby, you look hot! You want to hook up with me?" If you want a loving, long lasting relationship, it needs to be built on who you are as a person rather than physical appearance. Physical attraction is important in a relationship, but it should not be the center of the relationship. You will *not* look the same in those tight jeans when you're fifty years old. (See the chapter on relationships.)

We all love to receive compliments, but there is a substantial difference between compliments and flattery. Although some people may just be mimicking a negative role model, adults who flatter usually know exactly what they are doing, and it is for a selfish motive.

> We all love to receive compliments, but there is a difference between compliments and flattery.

How to give compliments:

1. Look at the person.
2. Speak with a clear, enthusiastic voice.
3. Praise the person's behavior. Be specific about what you like.
4. Use words such as "That's great," "Wonderful," or "That was awesome."

How to accept compliments:

1. Look at the person.
2. Use a pleasant tone of voice.
3. Thank the person sincerely for the compliment. Say "Thanks for noticing" or "I appreciate that."
4. Do not look away, mumble, or deny the compliment.

Sometimes people of faith wish to give all of the credit to God or other deity for their accomplishments. This can easily be interpreted as denying the compliment. In such a case, try and use words such as "Thank you, I've really been blessed."

Martial Hearts

Interactive Activity

Make two columns on a flip chart titled Compliments and Flattery. Have students call out things they've heard, said, or wish they could have heard. List them under the appropriate column. Discuss the differences and the feelings associated with each. Explain how we sometimes allow ourselves to be conned because it feels good in the beginning of a relationship, but later it becomes being treated like an object with no respected value.

Compliment	Flattery
That's a pretty dress.	You look hot in that dress.

Note: remember the difference is in the intent. It may be very difficult to discern the difference by the sentence alone. Example: "You look very nice today" is a compliment, unless it is repeated several times or for several days in a row. Excessive praise can be flattery. But many of us are so accustomed to such slang we have trouble discerning the difference between a compliment and flattery. We just don't see any harm in it. But these little things can lead to future problems. There may also be a case where a shy person wishes to befriend you, but either does not possess good social skills, fears rejection, or thinks you're so awesome that they choke up in your presence. You can usually tell when this is the case if you pay attention.

Asking for Help

We all need help from time to time. It may be in the form of assistance in accomplishing a task, borrowing a tool needed to complete a job, direction toward a specific goal, or advice concerning a situation.

Learning to ask for help appropriately is an important tool in establishing healthy boundaries. Two extremes to avoid are never asking for help, even when it's urgently needed, and being so needy that nothing can be accomplished without help. For more on this, see the chapter on boundaries.

Here is how to ask for help:

1. Get the person's attention without interrupting. Wait to be acknowledged. (See persons in conversation and school or business.)
2. Look at the person.

3. Use a pleasant tone of voice (girls, don't try to sound seductive as if you are going to go home with him if he helps you).
4. Ask for help using words such as "Please help me," "Would you be able to show me…?," "What can I do to…?," or "May I ask your advice?"
5. Listen to the person's answer. If it is long, write down notes so you don't forget.
6. Clarify anything on which you are unclear or did not understand. Say "I'm not sure I understand what you mean by that."
7. Thank the person for their time and help.

Interactive activity

Students role-play, asking for help appropriately from each other. Make a list of different suggestions from students in the class.

_____
_____
_____
_____
_____

Expressing Feelings Appropriately

Communication is extremely important in any relationship, whether it is male to female, student to teacher, sibling to sibling, or child to parent. When assumption is used to formulate an opinion, perception is rarely accurate. Lack of proper communication often destroys relationships. Look up the meaning of *assumption*, *formulate*, and *perception* to achieve a better understanding of the previous sentence. Then use your thesaurus to see what words might have been interchangeable and still come up with the same meaning. This will help increase your vocabulary, which will make you a better communicator.

For example: I once was in love with a lady who was in love with me. She, however, thought me to be a playboy with women (which I was not). So she told me how she felt, but that she believed in monogamy. Not knowing what that word meant, I assumed it meant dating around with other people. However, with my being too embarrassed to ask, I answered that I did not believe in it. We stopped seeing each other, and that was that. Lack of proper communication or lack of strong vocabulary caused the end of what might have been a great marriage. We both, however, moved on in the arena of romance.

Miscommunication begins early in life for most people. Quite often, it is because of assumption. For example: A boy asks a neighborhood girl if she wants to ride bikes together.

She, in her mind, may think it's because he has strong feelings for her. He, in his mind, may have asked because there were no neighborhood boys available to go riding. Girls are about feelings; boys are about actions (mostly).

Here are some steps to express your feelings appropriately:

1. Remain calm and relaxed.
2. Look at the person with whom you are speaking.
3. Describe the feelings you are having using appropriate words, such as "I feel unappreciated" rather than "I feel like dirt."
4. Avoid profanity or statements of blame.
5. Take responsibility for your own feelings. Here is an example of an extreme case: "You made me hit you. You think I like hurting you? If you would just do what I say, I wouldn't have hit you."
6. Thank the person for listening.

Examples of expressing feelings:

1. I feel embarrassed when you talk about me like I'm some object you own or some prize you've won.
2. I feel betrayed that you would discuss our confidential conversations with other people.
3. I feel ashamed that someone talked about you yesterday, and I participated in it just so they would like me.
4. I feel there is a lack of trust in our relationship after you lied to me about where you were Saturday night.

Interactive Activity

Have students sit back-to-back, one student with pen and paper, and one student with none. Give students an object to describe. The student with the pen and paper draws the object, then the other student describes the object. The point of the lesson is to practice good communication skills. Some people think in pictures, and some think in words. I find students can easily draw an object but have difficulty explaining the object with words.

Example: Man walking dog. More times than not, they draw a blank and cannot describe what they are seeing in their mind. But watch them go with just a little inspiration from the teacher: Was the man tall? Was it summer or winter? Was the street paved or graveled? Were there houses on the street? Was it even a street, or was it a field? Was it a big dog or a small dog? What type of dog was it? Now the student has that little nudge to inspire his or her creativity.

Have students pair up and practice describing something that makes them happy. Review as a group to help them understand how to describe what makes them happy. Example: a theme park. Help the student describe what it is about the theme park and describe their favorite ride or rides.

This exercise leads back into how we must practice explaining how we feel. We often find it difficult to say what we are thinking of (seeing) in our minds. This practice helps explaining sad as well as happy feelings.

Following Instructions

Performing a task may be beneficial to the person who is doing the work, or it may be beneficial to the person for whom the task is being performed, or

> An unfinished task can create confusion and disruption.

both. An unfinished task can create confusion and disruption in the accomplishment of a project for which the task was required. No task is too small when it prepares for a major function the following day.

Example 1

You are asked to set the chairs in a room into a specific pattern for an upcoming workshop. When the workshop presenter shows up and the task isn't completed, he or she may need to skip their much-needed materials preparation time in order to set up chairs for the presentation.

Example 2

You are asked to call everyone on a list to give important information. You get to the Ls before your time is up, and you need to leave. But you didn't contact your supervisor to tell them the task wasn't completed. The next day, everyone with a last name beginning with M through Z will still need to receive this information. Practicing following instructions helps in the development of good communication skills. Here are some simple steps to remember when given a task:

1. Look at the person (keep eye contact).
    a. Detailed tasks may require you to take notes.
2. Repeat the task and ask for any clarification or time frame.
3. Acknowledge that you understand by saying "Okay" or "I'm on it."
4. Do the task immediately.
5. Check back. Be sure the instructions were followed correctly or if anything needs to be changed. Sometimes tasks may change, and the person following the original directions was not informed of the change. Also, if the task is not going to be completely finished by the designated time, inform the appropriate person so they will be aware of the situation.

Here are several examples of benefits you receive from this exercise, labeled a, b, and c.

a. Homework assignments

Homework is not for the benefit of the teacher, it is rather for the benefit of the student. Let's say, for example, you're given a project assignment on Monday to be handed in on Friday. Waiting until Thursday to begin the work can cause the work to be incomplete for lack of time or sloppy due to a rushed job. Because we often think better in pictures (remember the man walking the dog), the project will help you learn more about the subject of the assignment. As the child's brain develops into an adult brain, teachers are trained to help you learn to think as an adult. Although playing video games in small amounts helps develop hand-and-eye coordination and is important in developing the brain, too much playing relaxes the eyes and will slow the learning process. You must participate in developing your brain to a grown-up way of thinking by practicing responsibility. This continuous affirmation of learned knowledge, along with practice of new material, gives youth power through immediate recall of information.

Repetition Strengthens and Confirms

This is a saying used in martial arts to explain why it is necessary to repeat learned techniques or behavior many times. It's called autonomic reflex. Movements must become so automatic that they happen without conscious thought. They may be so reflexive that they seem almost precognitive or even instinctive. Application to academics is the same. As tests of learning become more challenging and stimulating, the base understanding must be so ingrained into the cognitive processing that no apparent thought is require in

> It is important to know and understand the human body in order to maintain peak performance in sports.

order to proceed. This is why homework is so vitally important to the learning process.

For Sports Training

It is important to know and understand the human body in order to maintain a peak performance in sports and games. This is accomplished by extensive and continued knowledge development and academic study in the formative years of education. Remember that knowledge builds upon knowledge. Study of the human body will be extremely difficult without a strong working knowledge of language, math, and science.

For Self-Defense Training

It is explained that the brain controls the body. The brain sends signals to the body for response to defensive situations. For example: the brain will tell the arm to block a punch, or for the arms to fold properly when falling, thereby preventing a broken arm. Defensive responses also include situations such as a foul ball, or a fist headed toward your face.

This is where we get the wording *martial art*. Martial is *suggestive of war*. Art is an *expression of individuality*. In repetitive training, the brain intuitively tells the body how to react to given stresses. Thus, the martial art becomes the reflexes of the person. The person becomes the weapon (the art); indeed, they *are* the weapon. They have become an embodiment of the martial way (or life). Since we are all of different shapes and sizes, everyone can find a martial art that best benefits them at any age or stage of physical development. Long legs: tae kwon do; blind: hapkido, judo, or aikido; large framed: karate, wrestling, or just pick the bad guy up and chuck them across the room.

For Military Training

It is essential for military leadership to have a strong working knowledge of geography, social studies, language, and math. It is extremely helpful to know the terrain and exports of countries where one may be flown at a moment's notice for hostile environment insertion. For the individual combatant, it is imperative to quickly assess situations, which are stressful and dangerous. These include the recall of distance (x) rate/time to call in artillery on a moving convoy, or to calculate the velocity of a stream for fording with men, jeeps, tanks, etc.

In order to have quick responses to immediate danger, the brain must receive continuous stimulation. One way to continue positive brain stimulation during summer months is to read good books daily. Parental guidance and approval is recommended for the selection of reading material. For example: reading a book about relationships (or even studying *this* book) could help you advise a friend having problems with his girlfriend better than a book about a boy who became a witch. Also, excessive video game playing and television watching dull the brain processing, since it is relying primarily on the eyes. This makes it even more difficult for those with learning disabilities to process information in an educational environment. Drugs and alcohol destroy the brain. The question is still about where you want to be in ten or fifteen years from now.

b. Household contributions (chores)

Following instructions for work around the house is a great practice for entering the workforce with a healthy attitude toward representing others for profit. Youth can understand chores if they think of them as contributions to the household. For example: most youth may have few chores beyond cleaning their rooms. Although chores may extend to:

- Sweeping
- Mopping
- Mowing for older kids, picking up sticks for younger ones.
- Cooking for teens.
- Laundry when they've learned not to pour the entire box of soap into the machine (like I did). Oh, what a mess.

Make sure kids understand not to surprise you with breakfast or laundry. In fact, they shouldn't use anything that turns on or plugs in until they've been trained properly on how to use it. With age, more duties arise until they are able to take care of their own first apartment, townhome, duplex, or house.

When asking what contributions to the household are made by the parent, grandparent, or guardian, youth seldom seem to realize those contributions extend beyond feeding the pet.

I've yet to meet a youth who is required to clean his parent's room (although I'm sure they are out there). So we don't consider youth cleaning their own room as a contribution to the household. Now that the definition of contributions to the household has been defined, we begin to list the contributions of the parents:

- Food
- Clothes
- Shelter
- Toys
- Healthcare
- Taxi
- and more

> When youth start to understand that they really don't have it so bad, they may look for other ways to contribute to the household responsibilities.

What are some other contributions parents or guardians make? Write as many as you can, such as providing toys or bikes or skates, car (maybe).

_____
_____
_____
_____
_____

Most of us have never thought about those contributions just listed because they're done in love. Love, however, is not included as a contribution because it is a gift given without expectation of a desired response. If love is given expecting a certain result, then it is a bribe. See emotional con games.

When youth begin to understand they really don't have it so bad, they may look for other ways to contribute to the household responsibilities. It merits repeating that they should be warned not to take it upon themselves to cook, do laundry, or use any appliance or tool, which plugs in or turns on, until they have been properly trained by their parent/guardian. Such use could result in damaged appliances. But more importantly, it could harm the child. Youth should use their learned communication skills to ask adults what they could do to help. Find something for them to do. It makes them feel like they are part of the team.

This leads us back full circle in how to follow instructions so the youth can be sure they are performing the task safely and appropriately.

Make a list of contributions you could make to your household. It's okay to ask for suggestions or permission from parents or guardians.

Clean trash out of the car
Take the trash out

c. Auto maintenance

When young people begin to realize they are reaching the age of the driver's license, they may take a more avid interest in automobiles. This is a great time to begin teaching them how to check the oil and tires, etc. Even give them the responsibility of being sure that the family vehicle has proper fluid levels at all times. This will help with their sense of belonging and need, which reduces the risk of gang participation. It will also teach them responsibility, respect for property, and the much-needed skills of saving money on auto repair as they mature. Don't forget to keep checking the work yourself to be sure it was done.

Make an auto checklist for maintenance. Teach and have student/child go through the steps for you without assistance. Practicing patience yourself is the best way to teach children to practice it. Check their work regularly. Praise what they remembered, and gently remind them what they forgot. Do not reward honest effort with harsh criticism. Daughters as well as sons need to know this.

Check windshield wiper fluid

Check oil

Clothes to wear while pulling maintenance

Use jumper cables

Discuss types of oil choices

Forgetting to check the oil can result in cracking the engine block and costs as much as two thousand to three thousand dollars to replace. If you can't remember to do a simple school project, as in "homework assignments," should you be trusted to maintain the family vehicle? Again parents, check the work. Teenagers forget. Remember that the I-know statements don't always mean they know. Explain it anyway. It's okay to tell them you just want to be sure you covered it.

How to Accept Being Told No

We are all born selfish. That's why a two-year-old doesn't need to be taught how to grab a toy and scream "mine!" Without the proper social skills of communication and appropriate behavior, being denied can cause insecurity to erupt in actions ranging from depression to rage.

We *must* learn to understand the word "no" is a full sentence! Here are the steps of acceptance:

1. Look at the person.
2. Say "Okay."
3. Don't pout, shut down, or display anger.
4. Calmly ask for a reason if you really don't understand.
5. If you disagree, bring it up later. If you argue, you are not accepting their response. Remember how I handled the angry parent?

Martial Hearts

Here are some suggestions on how to *say* "no." Don't think your child is too young to be hearing this in today's world.

Statement 1: If you won't have sex with me, it means you don't really love me.

Answer 1: I care enough about you to make the right decision for both of us. And the answer is no. If you love me, you'll respect my decision to wait until I'm ready. I wanted them to wait until their wedding night. But that's my wish for them.

Statement 2: I took you to that concert and paid for everything. You owe me! At least give me a kiss and let me feel you up.

Answer 2: I don't owe you anything. I thought this evening was your gift to me. Obviously, this was not a gift, but a bribe. Take me home, and I'll go wake my dad up to pay you for half of the evening.

By the way, I am an adult and single. I have pledged myself to remain abstinent from sex until I marry again. I have women think I'm rejecting them and even starting rumors that I'm gay. I understand being a teenager, it's even worse.

Here is a situation to discuss *no* as an answer:

It's test day in math class, and you forgot to bring a pencil. The person sitting next to you has two pencils (they organized their backpack with an extra pencil in case theirs breaks during the test). Should you be upset with your neighbor if they do not let you borrow their extra pencil, forcing them to possibly be unprepared? Could you raise your hand (accepting your mistake) and ask your teacher for permission to ask if any students have enough extra pencils to let you borrow one?

Here is an example of explaining why an answer was no.

Question: Hey, can I borrow your PlayStation?

Answer: No.

Question: Is it okay for me to ask why you won't let me borrow it?

Answer: Because I don't have a PlayStation.

If the person asking to borrow the toy became angry and broke the friendship without knowing the other person didn't even own a PlayStation, the friendship would have been lost due to a misunderstanding and might have even caused a fight. The good communication skills you are learning here are very important for developing healthy relationships.

> *"My life has changed since I joined your class...the world needs more people like you."*
>
> Cary F.
> deaf college student

Interactive Activity

Have some of the youth role-play situations and interject different ways to say no. Have other persons practice accepting no as the definitive answer. Give input, as needed, for proper understanding of this skill. Review the activity as a group.

One of the hardest situations to accept no is when a relationship ends. It can be very hurtful and presents the temptations to try and get back together through manipulation, or to begin a campaign of slander against the other person in order to pay them back for the pain you feel.

Next, we will learn ways to break up without turning the whole ordeal into a big mess. Even if you are solid in your relationship or not in one at all, learn this material so you may be able to advise a friend struggling with a breakup.

Breaking Up

Here are some tips on breaking up:

- ➢ Don't jump right into another relationship just to stop the pain or to make the other person jealous. It's not fair to the new person.
- ➢ Speak only well of each other—or not at all (after the breakup).
- ➢ Attend parties and school affairs to develop new interests.
- ➢ Take some time to feel the pain. After that, don't isolate.
- ➢ Actively use positive energy. Start with something simple, such as making your bed, then by cleaning your room, then the bathroom. Then the house. Don't hammer, saw, or otherwise build things because the lack of concentration due to anger or frustration may cause injury or mistakes.
- ➢ Go jogging. You begin to feel better from the endorphin release. Endorphins are the body's natural pain reliever released through physical exercise. They

are sometimes referred to as getting a second wind. Then contact a trusted friend to go walking and talk. You can get your feelings out of your system.

- Don't write notes, send e-mails, or call the person.
- Don't ask friends to hook you back up, to pass along messages, or to keep tabs on what they are doing.
- Don't get involved in conversations concerning the breakup, even if someone else brings it up. Just change the subject or walk away.
- Get out of self-pity by helping others (community volunteer work).
- Use the time to develop a deeper spiritual relationship with God.

Read "The Harp" in the stories chapter. For more details on this subject, you may wish to purchase a copy of Dear Abby's book *Breaking Up—or What to Do With the Pieces*.

How to Express Empathy and Understanding of Others

Em-pa-thy *(ĕmp ə-thē) psychol. The power to appreciate the feeling or spirit of others.*

One valuable social trait is having empathy toward others. Although we may care about their feelings and wish for them to be pain-free, only when we have experienced their tragedy or hardship ourselves can we truly empathize with them. We may wish others to not experience hurt, but grieving is an important part of the healing process. Sometimes all we need do in order to be there for the other person is to just be there for the other person. Remember not to tell them how they should or should not feel.

Here are steps to take when a hurting person is sharing their feelings with you:

1. Look at the person.
2. Don't listen to them as you read, write, or work on a project.
3. Listen closely to the person's words. Try to understand what they are feeling.
4. Don't interrupt. Avoid telling them you know how they feel if you have never experienced what they are going through.
5. Don't fix (unless they ask you for advice).
6. Be sincere.
7. Tell them you are there for them anytime they need to vent.
8. Do not repeat to others what they tell you in confidence.
9. Read "Special Needs."

Donovan and his brother, Riley, lost their father in a sudden and tragic event. Their cousins brought them into their family, where they are deeply loved. Although their cousin, Aidan, cannot relate to the death of a parent, he can sympathize with them. He has accepted them into his family, where he loves and looks after them as little brothers. I have been able to witness what a wonderful big brother he is for them.

Sometimes, however, the hurt someone is going through may be the embarrassment of a mistake (like a harmful thing said during a breakup). In order to make a proper amends and find closure, they may need to make an apology. If they were the one hurt, they may need to practice forgiveness to find closure for their pain. Here are some steps on apologizing and accepting an apology.

How to Apologize

It shows character for a person to make amends for their wrong actions. Sometimes it may be magnified by someone being inappropriate toward you, and you reacted negatively. Your action, being wrong, may require that you make amends to that person. This does not mean you are making an admission of fault for the situation. It is accepting ownership of *your* part in the matter. However, if the aggressor is someone who uses emotional abuse as a form of control, an apology may only be used to cause further pain. In such a case, it may be better to say nothing. The important thing here is, would you make amends if it was not going to be used to cause further hurt to you? It is always good to have an older trusted person from whom you can ask advice.

If your amends is for something you stole, lost, or damaged, then it may be replaced. Look up the definition of the word *amend* to help understand how to proceed. Under normal circumstances of doing or saying something that hurts another person, here are some steps for making an apology:

1. Look at the person.
2. Use a serious, sincere tone of voice. Don't pout.
3. Begin by saying, "I was wrong to…"
4. Do not make excuses, rationalize, blame them for your action, or point out the other person's faults.
5. Shake hands if the other person is willing.

How to Accept an Apology

1. Look at the person.
2. Listen to them.
3. Remain calm. Refrain from sarcastic remarks or body language.
4. Thank them for making the apology. Understand how difficult that may have been for them. You can tell by their body language and remarks if they were sincere or just following an order to apologize. You may still want to thank them to help them learn that it's okay to try and make things right, even if it is extremely embarrassing.

5. Don't go telling everyone what was said. It's none of their business, and you may end up needing to make an apology of your own.
6. If you are willing, shake hands to show the other person you accept their apology.

Greeting Courtesy

Shaking Hands

When introduced to or greeting a friend, smile and offer your hand for a handshake. Shake hands firmly and for a short time. It is considered rude and intimidating to squeeze too tightly or to shake with a limp hand. In some countries, it is considered rude to look a senior in the eyes, but in the United States, it is perceived as untrustworthy to not look the other person in the eyes. Look at the person, but do not stare. This can make them feel uneasy. Prevent your hand from being squeezed too hard with the handshake by loosening your point finger (a self-defense technique).

If you offer your hand in friendship to a person and they refuse you, say nothing and lower your hand. This person may have a reason for not greeting or may simply not wish to be your friend. This can be embarrassing and surely is a self-esteem deflator, but remember that we are responsible only for ourselves and do not have the right to force ourselves on people who choose not to be polite in return. In some countries, people do not shake hands as they believe negative energy can be transferred through touch. Rarely would you attempt to force someone to shake hands.

This is actually a good opportunity for you to demonstrate integrity to those around you. Find the definition of *integrity* in your dictionary.

Dignitaries

Now that you understand shaking hands with one of your peers, we can move on to the social procedure of meeting dignitaries. Dignitaries are persons of some social influence or importance (ambassadors, elected officials, etc.). But my belief, and I hope you will share this belief with me, is that parents and teachers are social dignitaries. It is their job to mold and guide you into adulthood, and then to be available for you when you need advice. If you have no parents, or you have parents who are not emotionally supportive of you, a guardian or mentor can fill the position. A counselor, teacher, or trusted adult can assume the role of mentor. Girls, don't call an adult by his first name. Call him *mister* then name. You are not on the same emotional thought level, and you must be careful not to become emotionally romantic.

You should always rise when introduced to or greeting a lady or other dignitary, wait for that person to offer their hand before shaking. If they do not offer their hand, just smile and say a short

> You should always regard your parents, your friend's parents, school educators, and other adults as dignitaries.

greeting such as "nice to see you" or "nice to meet you." One suggestion for teens and young adults is to speak slowly, as many adults tend to lose hearing as they age, and you guys can talk pretty fast.

It is proper to respectfully acknowledge adults as you pass them or enter their classroom, unless they are engaged in conversation. As a martial arts master who teaches that we should always show respect, I can tell you I've felt hurt when black belt students would walk past me and not even look at me and smile to acknowledge my presence. This is considered a sign of disrespect, but it also helps demonstrate the premise of this book—that teens and young adults still need some mature adult guidance. We understand that teens sometimes have other things on their mind at the moment.

You should always, *always* open doors for other people when entering a building (even your peers) and be sure your door doesn't shut on someone when leaving. If they thank you, don't say "not a problem." I prefer to say "it's my pleasure." This is much more courteous. One of my pet peeves is when a waiter or waitress tells me "no problem." My first thought is, *Does that mean you wouldn't wait on me if it wasn't convenient?* Of course, I know they don't mean it that way, but perception is reality. To serve someone is a meaningful and honorable job and should instill pride in the one allowed to serve others.

Huggers

Some people are huggers, but some may use hugging instead of a handshake in order to enter the boundaries of space for setting up a con game. Practice your boundary skills for keeping strangers at a distance. Lead them instead to only shake hands until you know them better. If the person becomes angry or is insulted, you will know they just wanted to hold you in their arms. A person with such a loving nature that they wish to hug rather than shake hands will not be offended and will accept your request for them to respect your boundaries.

> Practice your boundary skills for keeping strangers at a distance.

No one has the right to touch you without your permission. And don't let them put you on a guilt trip because you refused them. That is a con! Don't feel sorry for them and give in, or it will lead to inappropriateness, such as wanting to get you alone in a room. Most rapes are committed by boyfriends and acquaintances. When confronted with this situation, simply raise your hands between the two of you and back up (if possible) while straightening your arms out between you. To lighten the situation, you may say something like "Whoa! Personal bubble invasion."

When meeting someone for the first time, it is helpful to repeat their name as often as possible in order to help you remember their name. Remembering names can be difficult if we have a tendency to not pay close attention or be easily distracted. This is especially true for those of us with attention deficit hyperactivity disorder (ADHD) or attention deficit disorder (ADD).

When someone remembers your name, it gives you a feeling of value. When you remember the name of someone else, it gives them that same sense of importance, and they respect you for that, helping your friendship blossom and grow.

> When someone remembers your name, it gives you a feeling of value.

It is always proper to rise to your feet when meeting or speaking with another person. Ladies are exempt from this rule and may greet others while seated if they choose to do so. This does not include women with jobs equal to their male counterparts, such as in the military. Do not tell a person they are being rude for not standing, as they may be recovering from an illness or injuries, which prevent them from rising easily.

Since I am a disabled veteran and am sometimes suffering pain in the knees, I will sometimes not stand when greeting someone. I always rise, however, when I am feeling well enough to do so or when meeting a dignitary. Also, you should always stand when a dignitary enters the room. This includes if they (including ladies) come to your table or wherever you are seated.

Practicing courtesy is fun. It is a sense of value and respect for yourself as well as others. It can also give a sense of adventure and excitement. I enjoy seeing the gleam in someone's eyes when they are treated with respect. There are courtesy rules for everything, even talking on the phone.

Phone Courtesy

When answering a telephone call, *smile* and use polite language. Words over the phone line may sound harsh since the person on the other end cannot see your body language. Smiling has a natural ability of making the voice sound pleasant, professional, and mature. It is difficult to sound rude while smiling without using sarcasm.

Avoid using short words, such as "what" or "huh?" Use phrases, such as "How may I help you?" or "May I ask who is calling?" This is much more polite than asking "Who are you?" or "What do you want?"

If you lay the phone down to get another person, be sure to tell the person on the other end of the phone that you will be right back or that you will go and get the person they are requesting. Don't just walk away leaving the other person to wonder what happened to you. Also, try to avoid setting the phone down hard against a table or cabinet top. The noise in the receiver is louder than you realize and may hurt the listener's eardrum.

When calling someone on the phone, the proper procedure is to identify yourself first and then ask for the person with whom you wish to speak. If you call the wrong number, don't hang up on the person who answers. Apologize to the person and explain that you must have dialed the wrong number. You may even repeat the number you are calling to see if you misdialed.

It is normally considered proper courtesy to phone people before 9:00 p.m. unless the specific party has given permission to do so, or if it is an emergency. This allows the family time to prepare for the night's sleep. If you must call someone after 9:00 p.m., begin your conversation with an apology for calling so late and explain your urgency. If it is not an emergency, ask the answering party if you have called too late. They may be fine with you calling at that hour, especially on a weekend.

You should always respect the amount of time you spend on the phone. Chat time should not last more than twenty minutes if you are using a parent's phone line. It is okay to set limits for your personal phone if you have long-winded friends, but be consistent with everyone who calls and ask them to respect your phone etiquette. Hanging up and calling right back may be a literal response to phone limits, but it is actually no different than staying on the line without hanging up.

If you call a friend's home and their parent tells you they are not there, do not continue to call every fifteen minutes for the next three hours. Ask when a good time would be to call back or ask when the parent expects them home. Then ask if you may either call back at that time or leave your number for them to call you.

Movie theaters are not the appropriate place for texting or checking your Facebook. It is very distracting to the people for several rows behind you when your cell phone is brighter than the movie screen or for those in front of you when you are talking during the movie. Although the movie theaters don't follow through with their threat to remove someone for this violation (they don't want to lose business), the moviegoers have started taking the matter into their own hands. For myself, I decided to just wait for the movies to come onto my television provider's pay channel and now rarely go to the theaters. You also should never have your phone out while driving an automobile.

Car Courtesy

It is extremely discourteous to pull up in front of a lady's home and honk the horn to let her know you're there. If you respect her, get out of the car and walk to her door. You don't need to have a lot of money to be a gentleman. Open the door for her when she is getting into or out of your car. Don't start trying to sound all uppity in your speech. Just be yourself.

You can tell her as you arrive at her house, "I'll get your door." Don't scold her if she opens it herself out of habit. In today's world, women are not accustomed to being around gentlemen, which is actually in

> When riding or driving a vehicle, it is not okay to slander the driving behavior of others on the road.

your favor unless you go acting a fool by trying to get her to be intimate with you. Don't try to con her. Ladies, be sure to set your boundaries and stick to them. Gentlemen, it's okay for you to set boundaries as well if you really respect yourself as well as your date.

When riding in or driving a vehicle, it is ungentlemanly (or unladylike) to slander the driving behavior of others on the road. Shouting, swerving, honking, and making hand gestures are signs of poor social skills and a lack of tolerance toward others. It is also disrespectful to your passengers.

Drinking alcohol or being on drugs while driving is dangerous. The loss of focus caused by the effects increases the chances of having a wreck and also implies that the safety of your passengers, those in other vehicles and pedestrians are not at the top of your concern as the person responsible for operating a motor vehicle. Talking on a cellphone is also extremely dangerous. Talking on a cell phone while driving increases your chances of having an accident by 350 percent, and texting while driving—well, that's just plain stupid.

Safety needs to be placed ahead of personal comfort. As the driver of a motor vehicle, you alone are responsible for the safety of others (this point deserves mentioning twice). When your friends get in the vehicle, you should make sure they put on their safety belts. I've heard that front seat riders can be killed by backseat riders being thrown

> Talking on a cell phone while driving increases your chances of having an accident by 350 percent.

forward. One way to encourage this action is to say, "Buckle up is a nice way to say I love you." Guys riding with guys, more than likely, are not going to say I love you, so another way of making sure everyone knows to buckle up when you're driving is to say something like, "Dudes, seat belts are involved." Watching for pedestrians is also the responsibility of drivers.

Walking Courtesy

When walking with a lady or a dignitary, it is proper for you to walk on the side closest to the traffic. On a sidewalk, you should still walk on the side closest to the street. This is a gesture of protection and care. If you are walking with a peer who wishes to take the outside, this suggests that your friend either has great respect for you, or he doesn't know about this and just happened to end up on the outside.

When approaching a closed door, it is proper to open the door and quickly glance in while moving out of the way for the person you are with to enter. This is to ensure the safety of the person entering that they are not about to walk into someone coming out, and that the area is clear of debris, water on the floor, etc. There are several times a day when someone is slightly hurt attempting to cross a threshold. It only takes a quick glance. You're not on a military reconnaissance mission. If you notice something unsafe, such as a crowd of people or a wet floor, you may gently take the lady's arm and escort her safely through or around the situation. Helping a lady around a slippery floor is especially important on formal occasions when she may be wearing slick shoes. It is not necessary, however, to take off your coat and lay it over the floor. If you are with a dignitary, such as your father, coach, or teacher, you may simply advise them to watch their step.

When entering a cased opening (an entryway with no door), it is proper to offer the lady or dignitary to proceed first. This is done by slightly nodding your head and laying your arm out forward and toward the ground with your palm open and upward. No words are needed for this gesture of courtesy.

If you are with a lady in a crowded room, you may need to take her hand or elbow and gently lead her through the crowd. This may most often happen at restaurants.

Dining Courtesy

A gentleman will pull the chair back for a lady to be seated. If not, at least allow the lady to be seated first. Dignitaries should also be seated first. This is not just in dining, but anytime you are seated. If a waiter is already seating the lady, you may put your hand on your chair, pulling it out slowly so that you will be sitting just after she is seated.

> Never chew your food with your mouth open.

It is extremely distasteful to chew with your mouth open, make chewing noises, or talk with food in your mouth. You should take your time while eating. Cut small pieces of meat, one at a time, and chew thoroughly before swallowing. Do not rush, yet do not drag time out picking at your food or talking so much that you don't have time to eat. When dining with a group, it is polite to finish with the slowest person eating. This slower-eating person will feel more comfortable since they are not being rushed, causing a delay in the evening's social agenda. (Remember to look words up in the dictionary to get the full meaning of words, such as *agenda*.)

Video games, phones, and iPods should never be brought to the table. Some families allow their children to play video games in order to keep them quiet and passive. This may make your evening more enjoyable, but your children are not learning proper social and table manners. Don't whine about your children not being mentored at school when that responsibility begins with you! Although times and customs have changed, it is still offensive to older generations to wear hats and caps indoors, especially at the table. However, it is not polite to inform strangers they are being rude by wearing their hats in a restaurant. Inside your home is a different matter. It is okay for you to ask someone to remove their hat at your table. However, if you are at the home of another, it is not your place to set rules for the host. They may have no problem with someone wearing a hat or cap in their home or even at their table. You, however, may remove yours to show respect.

Sit with your elbows off the table. Sit upright without slouching, holding your napkin in your left hand, and your left hand in your lap. Use your left hand to hold the fork while cutting food and either hand if something needs to be passed, such as salt. Set your plate close to the edge of the table and eat upright over your plate (not leaning over it). Lay your knife down after cutting. You may reverse the process if you are left-handed. Cut your food into small pieces and chew thoroughly. If the food is not pleasing to you, do not announce to the entire table that the food is no good. Do your best to eat some. Apologize to the host that you do not have an appetite for this particular serving. There may be something else to serve you.

Going Indoors

It is appropriate to remove your hat when going indoors. This does not apply to airports, hotels, and shopping malls, but certainly does apply to restaurants and houses. At your house, you may politely ask a guest if you may take their hat. Most people (especially cowboys) will say no. Then ask them if they would remove it since you prefer no hats be worn inside. You may lighten the mood by telling them (jokingly) they won't be needing to make a quick getaway. If they still refuse, don't make a scene, but insist they remove it for the prayer and throughout dinner. If they still refuse, simply allow them and don't invite them back. This person does not respect you.

Be sure to always check your shoes for cleanliness before entering someone's home or place of business. I remember a time, in Austin, when the yuppie crowd removed their shoes and put them on the porch and entry hall. This protects the carpet. If you wish to try this, remove your shoes and put them on the porch or in the entry way to set the trend. The host my appreciate it.

When entering through a door that is closed, be sure you do *not* leave the door open behind you. One common mistake is believing someone else is right behind you, only to find out they weren't coming in yet. Then whoever comes in next may assume the door was meant to be open and come in leaving the door still open. The same applies for leaving. Always be quick to offer your seat to ladies, the infirm, and the elderly. And, very important, one should never enter the bedroom of the opposite sex, even just to hang out. A lady never invites a gentleman into her bedroom, and a gentleman never enters a lady's bedroom, even if invited. It may seem harmless to you, but it is a good subject for rumors.

Persons in Conversation

Do not interrupt people in conversation, unless it is an emergency. Stand at the side of the person with whom you wish to speak, but a step back. This will alert them that you

> Always remove your hat when you enter someone's home or business.

wish to have their attention, but that you are not eavesdropping on their conversation. If they do not acknowledge you, wait for a break in the conversation and say, "Excuse me, may I have a word with you?" If they stop and turn toward you, acknowledging that you may speak, be sure to begin with "Excuse me for interrupting."

If at all possible, you should avoid walking between people while they are engaged in conversation. If you must do so, do so quickly, taking up as little time as possible and without speaking. Simply smile and nod as you pass.

School or Business

When approaching the door to a person's office, there is a proper procedure before entering. Look in while approaching to see if the person is in conference or on the phone. If the person is busy, wait patiently outside and away from the door or try again later. If the person appears to be available, knock lightly and ask if this is a convenient time for them to see you. When invited in, say, "Thank you for seeing me."

> There is a proper procedure for entering someone's office.

Discourteous People

If you see someone breaking a courtesy rule, avoid pointing out their flaw to them or to someone else where they can hear. This may be considered rude as we are responsible for our own actions and not for the actions of others. If it really bothers you, practice your breathing. If they are loud and vulgar, ask for another table. I must admit, however, that I once asked a young man if he ate with that dirty mouth. I was with a lady at the time, and she was becoming more and more uncomfortable.

Practicing these courtesy rules are fun. You will start to feel good about yourself because you are putting others first. To make sure others are comfortable is the definition of a gentleman or a lady. Being wealthy doesn't make you a gentleman or a lady; however, being a gentleman or a lady can make you wealthy—wealthy beyond measure, not with money, but with respect and contentment. You have this sense of feeling peaceful, serene, and happy inside and out. In this life, when so many people are so selfish and feel so empty, you are making a difference, a light in a world of darkness. You may be the only positive thing in their day. Who could ask for more?

See how much you remember about courtesy by answering these seven true-or-false statements:

1. _____ Always smile when answering the phone.
2. _____ Tell people to stand up when you are being introduced.
3. _____ Always squeeze hard when shaking hands.
4. _____ Video games should not be brought to the dinner table.
5. _____ Always remove your hat when entering someone's home.
6. _____ It is okay to interrupt people in conversation during an emergency.
7. _____ There is a proper procedure for entering a person's office.

Bonus statements:

8. _____ A gentleman never enters a lady's bedroom unless married.
9. _____ A lady never allows a male friend into her bedroom other than her husband.

(Answers on page 272.)

7
Basic Hygiene

Some people may think this subject needs no explanation. However, I have met many young people (and some adults) who did not understand basic hygiene. Even the basic concept of showering was unclear to them, causing them to be less presentable as a gentleman or lady. I once knew a man who for several years thought he had a hearing deficit but refused to see a doctor. He may have been too embarrassed. He spoke very loudly and was always asking others to repeat themselves. Finally, he went to an ear doctor and found the result of his hearing loss was that he had not cleaned inside his ears for more than thirty years. Once the massive cake of built-up dirt was removed, he was surprised how well he could hear. Below are four directions for basic hygiene.

a. Shower

Warm up the water. Step carefully into shower or bath. Get body wet, then soap body. In and behind the ears can be easily forgotten, but need cleaning. Thoroughly rub shampoo into scalp. Rinse and repeat. When drying off, never put anything in your ear larger than your little finger in a tissue or a piece of toilet paper.

b. Hands

Wash both hands thoroughly with warm soapy water, then rinse. When at businesses, leaving the rest room, remember that the doorknob is unsanitary. After drying your hands, use the paper towel to open the door. There should be a trash can near the door for this purpose. Spray all home door knobs regularly with disinfectant.

c. Toilet

When using the toilet, be sure you do not miss your target and make a mess for others to clean. Men should stand close enough to the toilet not to make a mess on the floor. After your bowels move (a number 2), flush toilet to prevent clogs when you send toilet paper down the drain. Do not use excessive handfuls of paper. When finished, flush the toilet! Leaving toilets without flushing them is very unsanitary. Wash hands and use the hand cleaning paper to turn off the water and to open the door.

d. Teeth

Brush your teeth when you wake up and before you go to bed. If possible, you should brush after every meal. Brush an up-and-down motion on your front teeth and don't forget the back of your teeth. You should also floss your teeth every day.

8

Proper Breathing Techniques

BREATHING IS SOMETHING we all do, of course, but a majority of us (in America) don't know how to breathe properly. Here is an explanation of proper breathing for you to learn and practice. Intentional practice will lead to automatic correct breathing.

It's normal for us to take a huge breath of air without utilizing our entire lung capacity. Watch someone take a deep breath and then have them watch you. If you see the chest rise immediately at the beginning of the breath, you'll know it was improper breathing. Do not use this as a con game to see or feel someone's stomach or breast. Have more respect for yourself and behave with some dignity.

Many people develop breathing problems because they breathe strictly from the top of the lungs, filling them

> Many people develop breathing problems because they breathe strictly from the top of their lungs.

downward with air. The proper way to take a full breath of air is to breathe just the opposite, from the bottom-up. If the entire lung is not used, it may become sick from nonuse. If you don't use it, you'll lose it, like with muscles.

Here is a way to begin practicing using your entire lung capacity:

1. Lay your hand flat against your stomach.
2. Push your hand out with your belly button as you breathe in deeply through your nose, filling the stomach and then your chest.
3. Allow the air to escape on its own through the mouth. Blow out what is left.

Now you have taken a complete breath.

There are many benefits to proper breathing. When you have a proper amount of oxygen in your lungs, it cleans the blood and feeds the muscles. You feel stronger, more energetic, and you increase your stamina.

When you feel angry, frustrated, or hyperactive, you can use this following technique to lower your heart rate and blood pressure as well as cool off your brain and reduce stress.

1. Breathe in as previously instructed.
2. While you are breathing in, think to yourself, *Blue*. Blue represents peace, such as still water. This is the calm coming into your body.

3. When you reach the top of your breath (lungs are full of air), think to yourself, *I am calm*.
4. Slowly blow out the air through your mouth.
5. While you are blowing out, think to yourself, *Red*. Red represents hostility, such as fire. This is the anger, frustration, hyperactivity, etc. leaving the body.
6. When you have let your air out, count the breath: one, two, three, etc.
7. Take about five slow breaths. More if you need to in starting the practice.

Side note for kids: hyperactivity means like when you can't be still or when you feel like you just have to do some type of movement and can't stop until you do.

We don't always recognize when we are being hyper, but adults will help us to know by the things they say (which is why it's so important to practice the listening skills we talked about in the front of the book).

> Parents and teachers will help us to know when we are being hyper. We just need to listen.

They may say things like "Calm down, now" or "Settle down." If we are being really hyper, they may say, "Will you chill out!" This is an indication that we need to sit down and practice our breathing. These learned skills can also be applied to relax and help you focus before a test or a big game. You need to remember this takes practice. Lots of practice, but it's worth it.

Without looking back through the book, see if you can jot down some things you learned from this chapter. Then go back and read it again and jot down some more things you learned during the second read.

_____

_____

_____

_____

_____

_____

_____

_____

9

The Difference Between Men and Women

WE ALL KNOW the obvious sexual differences between men and women. However, there are also differences which, although noticed, many of us don't understand the reason for the difference. Men are generally larger. Women generally (though not always) get cold easier. There are lots of differences, and we will discuss a few of them just to give you a basic understanding that it is a normal part of our human design from an intelligent creator.

In addition to the obvious differences, there are also many other inherent traits that can be seen. Have you ever noticed how men and women differ in action? Watch your friends and you'll see (most of the time) they will have consistent differences.

For example: when you tell men and women to look at their fingernails, men will hold their palm in front of them and curl their fingers to look specifically at the nails. Women, on the other hand (no pun intended), will straighten their arms out and look at the entire back of their hand and their nails as they relate to the hand and arm.

Another example is when men and women look at the bottom of their shoes. Men will cross their legs, pull their foot upside down in front of them and look at the bottom of the shoe. Women will generally hold their leg up behind them and look over their shoulder at the back of the leg and bottom of the shoe.

> Have you ever noticed how men and women differ in actions?

Still another example is the way they carry books. Men generally hold them in one hand at their side, while women hold them with both hands in front of them.

These traits are not accidental. There are four major differences between men and women. They are the brain, emotions, sex, and physiology.

The Brain

The brain is a wonderfully marvelous and complex major part of our body. A woman's brain has more receptors than a man's brain. I would think this means she can think faster. But men compartmentalize their different thoughts while women's thoughts are intermixed with emotions. It helps to think of it in a word picture. Men's brains have individual boxes while women's brains are like a bundle of wires, always touching, always firing. Men have all these little individual compartments or boxes in their brains to store topics, such as sports, education, cars, girls, etc. For women, everything is related and intertwined with feelings, situations, and circumstances.

Remember the examples previously mentioned about looking at the fingernails and shoes? No one taught us these traits. Right? Maybe boys look at just the nails and bottom of shoe because we are focused on that one thing, the nails or bottom of the shoe. That's where we were told to look. Women will generally look at their nails the way they do because they are looking at the nails as they relate to the entire look of the hand, or the shoe as it relates to the entire look for the foot and leg as well as how it will be perceived in public and by their friends and family.

Emotions

If you put young children in a room to play with toy cars, you can probably guess the outcome if you have children or siblings. The boys would generally race and wreck the cars while making tremendous crashing noises. The girls, however, would generally play family. "Get in the car, honey, we're going to the doctor. Don't worry, it won't hurt." Why is this?

Girls are relational. Everything connects, like a bundle of wires, always touching and firing. Boys are in their box—cars.

Sex

When it comes to sexual excitement, men and women are different in that respect as well. Men are stimulated visually, while women are emotionally stimulated. Men see skin, and they instantly get turned on. Women want to talk and cuddle and feel loved. Many men will display love in order to get sex, and many women will give sex in order to feel loved. But sex doesn't mean love, and love doesn't mean sex. Remember earlier in the book when we discussed your dreams and what could prevent them from coming true? Well, giving a false sense of your feelings in order to feel comforted or satisfied will not last. It is a distraction, just like having the unnecessary things in your backpack at school. You may assume everyone else is doing it, but wanting to be like others can prevent you from becoming what you want to be in life. This applies to boys as well as girls.

> Sex doesn't mean love, and love doesn't mean sex.

To have a successful, healthy relationship, a slow-building friendship is needed in the beginning. Men have a need to be admired and appreciated, and women need love, devotion, and understanding. These are the traits that can only be given when you know someone well, and that takes time. The con games section goes into more detail on this subject, but it also relates back to the hamburger or casserole chapter.

Physiology

Have you ever wondered why women get cold easier than men? Ever seen your mom and dad fight over the thermostat? That's another difference between the two sexes. Forty percent of a man's body weight is lean muscle while only twenty-three percent of a woman's body weight is lean muscle. This does *not* mean that women have more fat than men. The more lean muscle a person has, the more calories are burned. Calories are units of heat, which is why we use the term "burning calories." You may want to explain this knowledge to your parents if they begin to argue over the thermostat. This is not one hundred percent true for everyone, but for the majority.

Being different is a wonderful blessing, which enables us to give ourselves to someone completely rather than just physically. When we are dedicated to having our dreams come true, we will appreciate a partner who wants us to realize those dreams as much as we do and supports us in every area they can. Someone who only wants comfort for themselves will find it very difficult to nourish a relationship. They will become more of a dominator than a partner. We need to be in healthy relationships with others. So your next question is, "Great! So how do we do that?"

I'm so glad you asked. Read on.

10

Relationships

Re·la·tion·ship *(rĭ-lāshən-shĭp)* n. *The mutual exchange between two people or groups who have dealings with one another.*

THE KEY WORD in this definition is *mutual*. The dictionary doesn't divide the definition of relationship into healthy or unhealthy. According to *Webster's Dictionary*, if there is not a mutual exchange between two people, it is not even a relationship. A healthy relationship will include love, honor, and respect. Those which do not have these characteristics could be given a title other than that of a relationship.

Some people will disagree with the above statement since a person may merely display the traits of a mutual exchange for self-preservation. This, however, is fear, not love. This is why, on average in America, four million women are beaten by their partners, and three of those women are beaten to death every day. Every day! I used to think women in these positions should just leave. Well, I've been educated on the ignorance of that thinking.

An abused woman, whose husband reads her e-mails, checks the odometer in her car to be sure she hasn't driven too far, etc., has her in a bind. If she leaves him, he shows up at school and gets the kids. Then tells her to come home if she wants to see the kids again, and more and more horrible things, which prevent her from leaving.

> A healthy relationship will include love, honor and respect.

If you see red flags in a developing relationship, break up before it's too late. In the following chapters, you are going to read some things that may startle you, but you will read some things that I hope encourage and inspire you.

If you feel like one of the following, you may be in an unhealthy relationship.

> **Bondage**. Subjection to the constraint of duty or some strong desire.
> **Slave**. A person who is the property of another.
> **Hostage**. A person held as a pledge that certain conditions be fulfilled.
> **Maidservant**. A female servant.
> **Concubine**. A wife of inferior status.
> **Mistress**. A woman in relation to a man not her husband with whom she frequently has sexual relations.

If one or more of these definitions makes you feel anger, sadness, or embarrassment, it could mean that you are being convicted by a sense of guilt or shame due to the actions of yourself or someone you know. The good news is that you can change your situation, but you may need professional help to do so. It is often extremely difficult to break the hold that others develop over us. I know because I've been there. So I'm not speaking out of condemnation, but rather out of experience. That's why I know there is hope. After a failed murder attempt, I escaped that relationship, and so can you.

Listed below are attributes of healthy and unhealthy relationships. Put an *H* beside the healthy, and a *U* beside the unhealthy.

> **Gentle**. Not strong or violent, docile.
> **Patient**. Able to tolerate pain, troubles, difficulties, hardship, etc., without complaint or ill-temper.
> **Kind**. Pleasant or beneficial in action.
> **Jealous**. Valuing highly and guarding (God is a jealous God).
> **Jealousy**. A state of fear, suspicion, or envy caused by real or imagined threat or challenge to one's possessive instincts. It may be provoked by rivalry.
> **Rude**. Very impolite, vulgar, uncivilized.
> **Demand**. Claim as one's due.
> **Faith**. Trust, confidence.
> **Love**. A powerful emotion felt for another person, manifesting itself in deep affection, devotion, or sexual desire.

Don't be misled by the sexual desire part of the definition. Remember that sexual desire without idealized (shown in its perfect form) feelings is merely lust. Although sex is a part of love in a healthy married relationship, sex (in itself) does not mean love; sex means sex. Love lasts forever. Therefore, love will wait for the sex part until you are married. One of our society's controversies is whether or not people can have sex without getting pregnant or contracting disease. This battle has become a distraction to young people and the realization of their dreams.

> Abusers and con artists will try and rush the relationship.

Whether a young person does or does not experience the physical consequences of having sex, the emotional stress of broken hearts or in trying to maintain a relationship is one of the choices, which can prevent you from realizing your dreams. With so much pressure and responsibility on you concerning how you are having sex, does it not include a shred of intelligence to avoid these deeply emotional engagements until you receive your education and get into your field of choice, where you can make a positive difference while you're running the world? Shouldn't sex also be spiritual?

It sounds like such a simple thing to do, but the social pressure to fit in can be unbearable. So think about your future children. We know that most high school marriages fail. We also learned a proven statistic from the National Longitudinal Survey of Youth, which stated that nearly 80 percent of all children suffering long-term poverty come from failed relationships or unmarried families.

When it comes time to develop a mature and long-lasting relationship, we need to understand what love really means. What exactly is love? How do you describe it?

The best definition I found of love is that it is gentle, patient, and kind. Love is not jealous or boastful or proud or rude. Love does not demand its own way. Love is not irritable, and it keeps no record of when it has been wronged. It is never glad about injustice but rejoices whenever the truth wins out. Love never gives up, never loses faith, is always hopeful, and endures through every circumstance.

Meet Jay and Christine. They met while doing missionary work in Africa. Their first kiss was at the altar where they married in bare feet because the altar is holy ground. They now live happily with their beautiful children: Abigail, Gabriel, Isabel, and Nathaniel (with a fifth child on the way). I have the privilege of knowing them because Christine is one of my black belts. Jay and Christine are my inspiration. Since I have made a personal vow to remain abstinent from sex until God puts me together with the woman I would call wife, I think of them when lady friends of mine feel rejected at my denial for use of carnal knowledge. I have even had the rumor started that I am gay. It matters not when I think of this wonderful family and remember that I wish to give my wife the most valuable gift I have to offer—my spiritually, emotionally, and physically devoted love.

My recommendation for dating is to treat your date, as well as your friends, with the same respect that you hope your future spouse is being treated with on their date. This is done with the combined use of the skills you are learning in this book: boundaries, respect, modesty, etc. These and more are traits you need to practice for developing healthy relationships.

11

Developing Healthy Relationships

What is the term you would like to be described as "in a relationship"? Here are some options: girlfriend, boyfriend, main squeeze, hubby, paramour, live-in, significant other, old lady, sugar daddy, lover, better half, wife, and husband. How about this one: target. A male or a female who is setting up a relationship for selfish reasons will treat the other person more as a target than as a mutual friend. There will be times when you aren't sure about their odd behavior, or when they seem to have changed, but it's all part of the game, and they're playing you. They are also playing your friends and family to not believe you and to isolate you from supporters. What can you do to prevent this from happening?

Take time getting to know the person. I know I'm starting to sound like a broken record, but we need to hear something several times before the brain can remember something important, and this is important. Abusers and con artists will try to rush the relationship. They will isolate their "target" until there is no one to turn to for help. They will use phrases, such as "All you need is me" or "I'm the only one you can trust." In the con games portion, you'll learn one trick is to blame you. They may say something like, "If you loved me, then you wouldn't talk to them."

One of the difficulties in breaking away from an abuser is that you seem to have no one to turn to. It's as if they won't listen or don't believe you. But the game is being played on everyone. The player is not only grooming you for a desired behavior, but they will also be grooming others at the same time to believe them, rather than you. They may even have another person they are grooming for a relationship at the same time they are working on you. If you're taking time getting to know someone, and they inform you (or someone else) that you're not friendly enough, then you may have just saved yourself from an emotionally abusive relationship or from being used and dumped once they get in your pants.

So, again, take your time getting to know someone. Below is an activity that offers suggestions for taking time getting to know someone. These suggestions were made by youth.

Make two columns on a flip chart labeled as follows: What nourishes or builds relationships? What damages or destroys relationships? Let the students call out traits as you write them. When finished, point out how they are opposites.

Below are answers called out to me during a session I taught with high school students. It's amazing how honest they will become. They want this.

Nourishes Relationship	Damages or Destroys Relationship
Commitment	Noncommittal
Communicating well	Arguing
Respect	Abuse
Love	Lust
Accepting no	Forced sex
Trust	Untrustworthy
Responsibility	Secrets
Faithfulness	Cheating
Honesty	Lies
Tries to communicate well	Refuses to communicate

Now here are some suggestions for developing a healthy relationship before and during dating (courtship). These were also all written by youth.

1. Spend time with friends and family (not alone).
2. Take long walks and discuss hopes and dreams.
3. Take up a sport or other activity together.
4. Visit a religious worship together.
5. Take a younger sibling out for putt-putt and ice cream.
6. Make a scrapbook or Web site with other friends.
7. Cook dinner for your parents together.

8. Weed your grandparent's garden together.
9. Volunteer at a rape crisis center or family abuse center together.
10. Participate in fund-raisers together.
11. Have friends over for karaoke night (be willing to look silly).
12. Visit a veterans hospital or retirement home together.

Getting to know someone with whom you may wish to spend the rest of your life is vital in a relationship. Although physical attraction is important, it cannot be the main driving force in a successful marriage. For example: When I was twenty-five years old and fresh out of the Marines, I had some muscles and was cute. Now, at almost sixty, I can guarantee you don't want to see this body in a Speedo.

Nurturing a relationship can even move into the spiritual realm.

12
Spirituality

IN ORDER TO have a healthy relationship with another person, it is a necessary first step to have a healthy relationship with oneself. In order to best understand ourselves, we may wish to seek some sort of spiritual understanding.

No one has the right to tell you what or how to believe. But if you seek to gain knowledge of a loving and caring spiritual power, you may find a personal belief, which the two of you can share. With true spirituality comes wisdom. Example:

> True knowledge is not attained by thinking. It is what you are; it is what you become. (Sri Aurobindo)
>
> Seek ye first the kingdom of God, and everything else will be added unto you. (Jesus Christ)
>
> To be sorry for one's errors is like opening the door to heaven. (Hazrat Inayat Khan)

> Oh Great Spirit, make me ever ready to come to you with clean hands and straight eyes, so when life fades as a fading sunset, my spirit may come to you without shame. (Yellow Lark)
>
> What a source of consolation to know that even the sufferings and adversaries which God sends us are for our own very best, and have in view our eternal salvation. (St. Alphonsus Liguori)
>
> For it is in our lives, and not from our words that our religion must be read. (Thomas Jefferson)
>
> I bow to God, who lives in this world within us. Whoever calls Him by any name, by that name does He come. (Mahabharata)
>
> Calm down; be still, turn inward to the One True God who dwells within you. (The Holy Bible)

Being emotionally healthy ourselves, we can more easily help others understand the limits of contact for moving into the next level of romantic interest. This is called setting boundaries.

13

Boundaries

Bound-a-ry (*boundə-rē,-drē*) *pl.* **bound-a-ries** *n. the real or understood line marking a limit.*

A BOUNDARY IS the healthy emotional and physical distance between other people and ourselves. A boundary is important because it defines areas of privacy. It is like a chain-link fence, needing flexibility with an absolute point, which may not be crossed. But emotions have no chain-link fence and can thereby be crossed if allowed or forced. Initially, parents help you begin understanding boundaries as you see how far the chain-link fence will bend (so to speak). Later, you take a more active role in setting your boundaries.

There are two types of boundaries: external and internal boundaries.

> Setting and keeping boundaries will help us find true intimacy

External boundaries protect your body. Internal boundaries protect your emotions and your essence.

External Boundaries

There are two types of external boundaries:

Physical external boundaries protect you from direct attacks, such as rape, bullies, abduction and murder.

Sexual external boundaries protect you from unwanted personal advances, such as touching, fondling, exposing, oral sex, and sexual intercourse.

Internal Boundaries

There are two types of internal boundaries:

Emotional internal boundaries protect feelings, such as joy, sadness, depression, and acceptance.

> A boundary is important because it defines areas of privacy

Spiritual internal boundaries protect the essence of who you are, such as hope, trust, security, and your personal religious faith.

Boundaries of Space

There are three basic physical spaces for boundaries:

1. Stranger distance is full arm's distance.
2. Friend space (coworkers, classmates) is elbow distance.

3. Intimate space (spouse, family) is no daylight between you.

How do you know if your boundaries are appropriate? Boundaries that are too open:

- Shares too much personal information too quickly.
- Takes responsibility for other people's feelings.
- Believes they deserve bad treatment.
- Can't see flaws in others.
- Wears seductive or revealing clothing (includes sagging pants and exposed bra straps).
- Sits or stands too close to others.
- Has sex with strangers or acquaintances.
- Trusts strangers.
- Believes everything they hear.
- Can't say no.
- Makes sexual jokes.
- Makes bodily noises in public.
- Believes e-mail forwards are all true.
- Lists personal facts on Internet.

To read reports on abductions of young women and girls who have been sold into human sex trafficking operations, visit the website of the FBI (www.fbi.gov) or the Bureau of Justice Statistics (www.bjs.gov).

Boundaries that are too closed:

- Shares little or no personal information.
- Says no to any request.
- Cannot identify their own wants, needs, or feelings.
- Few or no close friends.
- Refuses help from trusted adults.
- Doesn't ask for help.
- Doesn't report sexual assaults.
- Will not shake hands.

Finding a balance of boundaries takes time, practice, and *qualified counseling*.

Signs that someone is crossing boundaries:

- Interrupts conversation.
- Is constantly correcting others.
- Takes personal possessions without owner's permission.
- Teases or makes fun of others.
- Asks personal questions.
- Gossips.
- Touches without permission.
- Reveals personal information about self and others.
- Doesn't respect personal space.
- Uses vulgar language in the presence of others.
- Forces someone to do something sexual.
- Intentionally hurts someone.
- Starts off playing and becomes more and more aggressive.

➢ Excessive questioning.

You may be able to think of more on this touchy topic.

Have you ever crossed a boundary?

Have you ever touched, pinched, or grabbed someone who did not want you to touch them?

Do you make sexual gestures, looks, comments, or jokes in public?

Have you ever sent someone unwelcome sexual notes, pictures, or e-mails?

Have you ever publicly put down or humiliated someone?

Do you reveal private information about others?

Do you stand or sit too close to others?

Do you raise your voice to stop someone else from talking?

Do you believe sex is a duty that a wife *must* perform whenever the husband wants?

Have you ever given someone a gift and expected something in return?

Have you ever treated your girlfriend/boyfriend like an object you owned?

Have you ever insisted on seeing your gf/bf's cell phone so you can see who they've been talking to?

Do you try to make other people seem less important than you?

Do you believe if a girl really loves you, she'll have sex with you?

Do you drop something so a girl will bend over where you can look down her top?

Have you ever bent over so a boy could look down your top?

Have you used sex to get something you wanted or to make someone jealous?

Do you believe you owe your date sex for buying your dinner?

Did you answer yes to any of these questions? If so, then you've crossed a boundary.

One good rule of thumb to help young people develop a healthy sense of boundaries is the *no sun rule*. Learning the no sun rule is simply understanding that if the sun doesn't touch it, no one does. Bathing suits are good examples, although some ladies' bathing suits expose areas, which are off limits to normal touch. It should also be explained that this doesn't apply to a doctor (in the doctor's office) or hospital performing an examination. Love, secrets, and threats are not valid reasons for private touching. The child should tell their mother, father, or school counselor. I once told a group of young people this, and if harm to them or their family was threatened, they could tell me because they knew no one could hurt me, and I would protect them. That night, one of the children told his father that his ex's father had been touching him inappropriately and threatening to harm his family if he told anyone.

Setting and keeping our boundaries will help us find true intimacy with someone whom we can share our desired adult lifestyle and goals. But what is true intimacy all about? The next chapter will explain this. First, I'd like to step out of format to explain again why this is so important, especially to females.

At the beginning of this page, I used the term rule of thumb. I believe this is important since we are including the abuse of women in our society. The term rule of thumb came from our legal system, which stated that a man could not beat his wife with a stick thicker than his thumb. There are still unequal laws in Texas. For example: a woman who kills her husband in self-defense will go to prison twice as long as a man who kills his wife in anger.

I know that's not fair, but it will continue to be one-sided until more women can stay in school and become professionals who can change these laws. You may be the man or lady who brings this much-needed change to our society. Socializing is important, but even more important is your education. Focus on learning, and you will become even more popular. Then, when you get out into the world and make a difference, you will be more than just popular. You will be famous. But the real glory is the fact that you will be helping women find equality in the legal system.

Now we move on to a lesson on intimacy.

14

Intimacy

Intimate (ĭnt ə–mĭt)

1. *Pertaining to the inmost character of a thing; fundamental; essential*
2. *Most private or personal*
3. *Closely acquainted or associated; very familiar*
4. *Promoting a feeling of privacy, coziness, romance, etc.*
5. *Resulting from careful study or investigation; thorough*
6. *Having illicit sexual relations*

NOTICE THE ORDER of definitions of the word in italics listed above. It begins with our own personal character, having a perception of ourselves as we see ourselves. The definition then progresses to basic friendships, to close friendships, to very personal friendships, to a physical relationship.

Knowing the differences in the sexes and practicing the basic social skills explained in earlier chapters, we become better equipped to engage in the friendships, which will let us get to know each other on a personal level. It is from these relationships we discover our compatibility with others.

Intimate personal details of thought or actions disclosed too early in a friendship may become gossip if the friendship ends. Intimate physical relations given too early in a friendship may cause emptiness inside if that relationship ends. Most relationships that enter into the sexual relation early in the friendship don't last. This isn't true for teenagers alone. More adults than ever before are now experiencing unsuccessful relationships. Wanting to have a healthy relationship requires the act of being pure.

Remaining pure can be achieved easier if we first understand what being pure actually means. So let's go to the dictionary.

15

Purity

Purity *(pyūrĭ-tē) n. the state or quality of being pure.*

Pure *(pyūr) chast*

Chaste (chāst) adj. *innocent of immoral sexual intercourse ‖ deliberately abstaining from sexual intercourse ‖ (of manner, speech, dress etc.) modest, restrained ‖ (Of literary or artistic style) pure, unadorned*

PURITY DOESN'T ONLY mean refraining from sex. It also means modesty in dress, speech, and behavior. Wow! Does that bring a new and better understanding of what it takes to remain true to your adult life (refer back to "Planning Your Future") and to that of your future spouse and children? You bet it does.

> Purity is the result of continued spiritual harmony with God.

Here are some examples of impurity (you finish the list):

Sexual body language	Wearing excessive makeup or jewelry
Revealing bra straps	Suggestive, written correspondence
Working in seductive clothing	Rubbing your body against someone
Working at a gentleman's club	Sexual gestures; vulgar or sexual language
Visiting a gentleman's club	Causing attraction to your body
Wearing sagging pants	Getting drunk in public
_____	_____
_____	_____

We can all be vulnerable to addictions, which cause us difficult struggles with being pure. One huge problem is pornography, which may start, believe it or not, with youngsters looking at underwear models in store shopping catalogs. It then can progress to nude photos in magazines, and then on to their younger sister, a friend's younger sister, or neighborhood youth.

Television and many hotels offer pornography, and parents must code in a block to protect their children. I believe a law should be passed so pornography does *not* come with the channel and must be coded in to receive it. Sadly, I've been told these channels bring in more revenue than any other. Today's Internet access is also too often a quick catalyst into the world of pornography. The next chapter explains this in more detail.

16

The Brain Needs More, Not Less

ADDICTIONS, SUCH AS pornography, can begin with a glance, move to a stare, and develop into a seemingly unbreakable habit. That's because the brain needs to be stimulated and challenged for growth.

Ask a fifth grader if they'd like to go to fourth grade, and they may say "sure" because it will be easy. But they will quickly change their mind when you explain that now they would be there all day, every day with those immature kids. They wouldn't be happy because it would quickly become boring and dull. The brain needs to be challenged, stimulated. It needs more, not less.

Boys can start with looking at pictures in a book of young shapely girls in their underwear. Those pictures will stop exciting them, and they will need to progress to pictures of thin shapely girls wearing no clothes at all. At this point, a problem begins to occur in the human brain. The picture of these young girls will remain ingrained in the memory without changing. You don't see these young ladies age into beautiful older women. That's because they are replaced by new young models in the magazines and on the Internet.

When these young men grow older, the physical stimulation in their relationship will fade because no woman in the world can continue to match the concept of sexual beauty he has ingrained into his mind. This will cause the boy much hardship and frustration when he is older. And, as a man, he may always seek out younger women.

There is another concern when pictures in books or on the Internet stop working to satisfy the brain's need for stimulation. Boys and men may become so obsessed with keeping that addiction fed they will start looking for females to satisfy their desire (or lust). To satisfy their lust, they may turn to their sister or a friend's sister, a neighbor, or a girlfriend from school. As children mature into adulthood, the need for satisfaction grows with them. Remember, the brain needs more, not less.

That's when many men begin forcing sex or raping women. Then it gets worse. Some murder their victims to prevent being caught. This can create a whole new unhealthy addiction. Many will also begin molesting young girls and threatening them not to tell. Some molesters even convince the girls that it was their fault because there may be a small degree of physical pleasure. However, other women who speak out about being raped themselves say there is no pleasure at all in the pain of a brutal sexual assault. Rape is not a crime of passion, but a crime of violence. Rape (or sexual assault to the politically correct) wounds its victims, many for the rest of their lives.

I once read that a rapist and mass murderer of women said his addiction began with adult magazines. You may think this could never happen to you, and I hope you're right. I really do hope you are not the one in four women who will experience domestic violence in your lifetime. But that just makes the stakes higher that your daughter, sister, best friend, or even your mother will experience it. Sex is meant to be a beautiful, God-given experience, but when it is abused, it becomes a lifelong injury.

No Man Is an Island

We men need to not only guard ourselves from such unhealthy behaviors, but we have an obligation to hold each other accountable for the consequences of our actions. Remember, iron sharpens iron. But holding each other accountable means we must allow another man to hold us accountable. If we don't, these addictions can become obsessions, and the behavior will be sought through con games. I found this to be mostly challenging with church leaders. Some church deacons and pastors have given me the impression that they are above sin due to their standing in the church. They must often manipulate and con others to keep their real actions hidden. This brings us to our next chapter, "Emotional Con Games."

One of my confidants is a brother in spirit whom I live near. We are completely honest with each other and hold nothing against the other for our honesty.

17

Emotional Con Games

What is a Con Game?

CON REFERS TO the word *confidence*. A con man is one who quickly gains your confidence and then betrays your trust. We normally think of a fast-talking salesman cheating grandma out of her life savings. In this context, however, we are talking about people who gain your confidence, then betray your trust in a self-gratifying moment of personal satisfaction. Whether these self-serving desires are based on money, sex, pride, status, ego, power, or other reasons, it is total control that the abuser seeks, and sex is often involved. In these cases, control is used for sex, or sex is used to control. It is, however, only a con if the woman is innocent, as

> It is easy for us, as a society, to blame the action on bad parenting and role models.

opposed to the one who plays the victim or is herself the con artist.

Those who commit these emotional abuses may or may not be consciously aware they are participating in a con. These traits can be learned or mimicked by imitating mentors and role models. Parents, older siblings, celebrities, and television characters are much to blame for demonstrating behaviors, which pattern the lifestyles of others. However, once a person has been made aware of their actions, the continued behavior is no longer innocent.

It is easy for us, as a society, to blame the action on bad parenting, teachers, and role models. However, if we are honest enough in the reading of this material to recognize that we all have picked up some of these traits to one degree or another, then we can begin to realize the enormity of the condition that we, as a society, are facing. The biggest threats to solving this problem seem to be:

1. Those who embrace this conning lifestyle to meet their own selfish wants with no desire to change.
2. Those who refuse to search their own true motives and insist they are innocent.
3. Those who believe in using any tactic which, in their minds, is for the greater good as they see it. The end justifies the means.

There are nine particular tactics, which an emotional con artist may use, to trap his or her prey. These are jealousy and possessiveness, insecurity, intimidation, anger, accusations, flattery, status, bribery, and control.

The "player" or "groomer" may use any one of these tactics, a combination of these tactics, or even all of these tactics, to gain control of his or her target.

The book *Unmasking Sexual Con Games* of the Boys and Girls Town was the main source of research for this material. Information on how to receive this and other related materials can be found in the acknowledgements section of this book.

> Every day, four women are murdered by boyfriends or husbands.

Age Does Matter

I once asked a ten-year-old girl, "Would you date a boy who was fifteen?" "Yes!" she replied quickly. "Would you date a boy who was five?" "No way!" she replied just as quickly. I went on to explain how she could easily get a five-year-old to do whatever she wanted and make him think it was his idea. The girl agreed. Then I explained how a fifteen-year-old boy could do the very same thing to her, and she would never realize that she had been manipulated. Her comment then was that she didn't know she was going to get a lecture.

If you are in high school or younger, you should not be dating a boy who is more than two years older than yourself.

Jealousy and Possessiveness

Although it is a fairly normal emotion to be jealous and to be possessive, when it is used to control or manipulate someone, it becomes part of the abusive con game. Remember the *Snow White* story of the jealous queen? She couldn't stand that someone could be more appealing to men than herself. There is a healthy desire to protect, such as God's love to keep His children in fellowship with Him. But that's a different topic. Here are some examples of jealousy and possessiveness used to manipulate and con by males and females alike:

Acts out in a jealous rage.

Monitors e-mails, phone calls, text messages and/or caller ID.

Opens mail.

Spreads vicious rumors about you or others.

Checks odometer.

Controls friendships.

Attempts to emotionally or physically hurt someone of whom they are jealous.

Controls dress, behavior, money, hairstyle, etc.

An example of jealous/possessive language is the statement "You belong to me."

We often try to handle these situations alone, which can only make the con more emboldened. Trusted or trained adults (such as counselors) can give extremely valuable advice and assistance in handling matters such as these before they worsen.

That is if the person hasn't already been groomed by your abuser.

Name–Claim–Tame

Just about everyone feels jealous at one time or another, so how do we control it when we are the ones being jealous?

Name. Ask yourself why you are jealous. You can be honest since this is for your eyes only. Write down feelings, situations, and people involved with the situation and try to realize if it is because you have a fear of losing something. Most situations of jealousy stem from fear of losing something. It could be fear of losing the relationship, popularity, money, security, etc. Your fear may be justified if the other person is, for example, always flirting with members of the opposite sex or spending long periods of time with his or her ex. Once you have named the reason for your feeling jealous, you can move on to the next step.

Make a list below of things that make you jealous and things you do, which make other people jealous. And if they were innocent or planned. Be honest with yourself.

_____

_____

_____

_____

_____

_____

Claim. Accept this feeling as being your problem and not that of the other person involved. If the other person is flirty, it may mean that you are the only one in a serious relationship. If you are the target of the jealousy, you must accept that it is his or her problem and not yours. You cannot change the insecurities of the other person by making yourself a prisoner to them, just as you cannot change your own insecurities by making the other person your prisoner. Either way, it's time to have an honest discussion about staying together or breaking up.

Write down what needs to be discussed.

_____

_____

_____

_____

_____

_____

Tame. Express your feelings as discussed in the chapter on social skills. It may be you need to practice trusting this person in the situations that make you jealous, or it may be that the other person needs to trust you. One of you may be trying to make the other jealous, and the ploy is working. Or it may be that the relationship is not serious and needs to be kept at, or moved back to, the friendship-only level. If these situations don't apply to you, write down situations you have noticed where other people have become jealous or made someone jealous. It will be good practice to prevent it from happening to you in the future.

Insecurity

Just like jealousy, insecurity is a normal emotion. Again, when it is used to manipulate someone else, it becomes a con game tactic.

Insecure people are all around us, trying to compensate for what they feel is a lack of adequacy. In martial arts, we see the guys who are always bragging about how good they are at fighting. The sad thing is that many of them are really good, but they have trouble accepting that everyone can be beaten at one time or another. Some of them create false resumes of championship titles and teach their students to lie about their ranking and age in tournaments in order to win trophies. Most instructors, however, are teaching integrity and honor as more than just words on a test.

When we stand firm against one con, the groomer may switch to a different tactic. For example: if you don't allow him to "bribe" you into sex because he paid for your dinner, he may call later with the "insecure" angle and give you his sad story of loneliness. When he does, tell him to buy a dog. Then again, it could be the girl who is the manipulator who makes a man spend money on her to earn her lovin'.

My Own Story of Insecurity

I remember in junior high school when I bought a pair of lifts to go in the heels of my shoes to make me look taller (I was very insecure about my lack of height). One of my family members innocently chuckled at me for it, but my older brother, with whom I was always fighting, told me that I didn't need to be tall to be a big person. That was a golden nugget moment for me and helped me more than any therapist could have. To this day, my big brother is still one of my heroes. I still pass that message along to youth who are experiencing the same feelings that I had those many years ago.

> Manipulating another person's insecurities is a way to control their thoughts and feelings.

If you have a story that someday will inspire a child who will idealize you, write that story on the next page. Journaling is a very healthy activity. Some people have even made a lot of money in later years because they wrote about what was happening during that particular period. Be bold, write your experience.

How Do You Recognize Insecurity?

As indicated above, behavior (or action) as well as words will show insecurity in a relationship. This is one reason why it is important to take your time getting to know someone. Don't just listen to what they say, but watch what they do. Do they walk the walk or just talk the talk? Be wary of people who are always going to do something and then don't, or are always promising something without following through by keeping the promise. And *don't* let them rush the relationship.

Here are some examples of things that insecure people may say in a relationship: "I'm not worth it," "I don't deserve you," "I'm no good without you," "I'll kill myself if you leave me," "I'd have nothing to live for," "Say goodbye to the sun for me because I won't be here to see it." And eventually, "If I can't have you, nobody will."

> Seventy percent of men who batter their partners either sexually or physically abuse their children.

Another way to use insecurity as a con is to magnify or create insecurities in the target. This manipulation of another person's insecurities is a way to control their thoughts and feelings. Some of these expressions may be: "No one else will ever want you," "Nobody likes you," "Everyone else thinks you're fat," and "When I'm through with you, you'll never be happy with anyone else."

So what do you do if you are beginning to experience this behavior? Talk to someone. Your parents, a counselor, or trusted adult are the most likely avenues of receiving the best help in resolving the situation before it worsens. If it's already bad, that is all the more reason to speak with someone without delay. Although friends are normally the first choice, remember that they may have already been groomed and may not seem helpful to you. An outside source, such as the previously mentioned counselor, may be the next step. Don't give in and don't give up. You may just need affirmation from an expert (or maybe someone who has been where you are now). Your parents should always be your first choice, unless they are emotionally detached from you.

You might even ask your mom or dad if you can see a professional without them demanding to know what for. Just tell them you'd feel more comfortable discussing it with someone you don't know.

Recognizing and owning (admitting to ourselves) our insecurities is a step toward dealing with them. It may be worry over money, fear of failure, or fear of success, being uncomfortable in large crowds, giving a speech in front of others, being fat, being skinny, being tall, or being short. It could be anything that is holding you back. Dealing with an insecurity now will make it easier to ask for help in an abusive or potentially abusive relationship so you can move on with your life. I must say now that all relationships are not abusive. I don't want to scare you to the point that you never let anyone into your heart. These are all worst case scenarios.

> Professional therapy is a proven method of overcoming the paralyzing trauma of emotional abuse.

Make a list of your own insecurities:

_____

_____

_____

_____

_____

Insecurity may feed other grooming tactics, such as intimidation.

Intimidation

Unlike the previously mentioned traits, intimidation is not a normal human emotion and has no place in a relationship. That is, if you want a healthy relationship. Some examples of intimidation are frightening behavior, force, threats, coercion, overpowering body language, becoming louder than the other person speaking, yelling, and vulgar or demeaning language.

Make a list of other ways in which people can be intimidated.

_____

_____

_____

_____

_____

If intimidation is tolerated, it will lead to a hostage situation in which you may feel unable to escape, and the relationship should be ended as quickly as possible. Often, when leaving a relationship, counseling and even self-defense lessons are needed. I've had two ladies that I know of take a self-defense class just out of interest, and their boyfriend or husband would ask them to demonstrate what they learned, and then hurt them, and the lady would quit. I would think the man may not even know he was intimidating her. But then, I would wonder why any caring person would not want his woman to learn how to protect herself?

So how do you escape this trap? Talk to someone. Don't allow threats of hurting others prevent you from seeking help. Others will be hurt enough emotionally just seeing you suffer this abuse. They may fear offering advice without being asked since it could be interfering.

Make a list of acts that have intimidated you. Make another list of acts where you have intimidated others. Be honest with yourself and then compare the lists. People who are often bullied have a high risk of becoming a bully themselves.

Intimidation can lead to anger, then rage. For example:
"Shut that kid up!"
"Don't make me hit you again!"
"I'll f—ing kill you bitch!"
Can you name something you or someone else may have heard?

_____
_____
_____
_____
_____
_____
_____

Anger

Anger is another normal emotion. What we do with that feeling determines positive or negative outcomes (whether we use it right or wrong.) An example of using anger for a positive outcome is what we term *righteous indignation*. There is a story (I haven't verified if it is authentic) about a rapist/murderer called "The Boston Strangler." The story speaks of a former marine who would intimidate women in a park by grabbing and threatening them to do whatever he wanted without resistance. He would then rape them, and when he was finished, he would murder them so there would be no witness. One woman had worked hard and saved her money for a new leather jacket. He threw her onto the ground, and she was giving in to his demands until she realized that it was damaging her new leather jacket. She became so angry that she fought back and screamed. The attacker ran away from fear of people hearing the screams and was arrested and identified. Anger used in conning is what the strangler used on his victims until this one lady's righteous indignation. There has become such a lack of value for human life that self-defense instructors are teaching "comply and die!"

> Domestic violence is the number one cause of emergency room visits by women.

Anger to manipulate is abusive behavior. Angry outbursts are a way to "control." If we allow this behavior to continue, there is only one outcome—the situation will get worse! The reason it is dangerous for the victim or target is because the brain needs more, not less. The brain needs to be stimulated constantly. It will accept newly introduced information (if repeatedly entered) as normal, and then the brain is ready for that information to be increased. Remember the example in "The Brain Needs More, Not Less"? It stated how the brain needs to be challenged, stimulated.

When violence is accepted in the smallest degree, that acceptance makes it easier for the brain to then think of the abuse as normal. Excuses, such as "at least he doesn't hit me" will become "at least he doesn't hit the children." These rationalizations often progress into making excuses as to how family members received new bruises and even broken arms or legs.

> There is no such thing as missional dating.

Yelling will turn to grabbing; grabbing will turn to hitting and then beating. But anger doesn't always manifest itself physically. Emotional abusers (such as some preachers and retired military) will suppress their victim to the point of having no self-esteem or freedom whatsoever. Passive aggressive behavior is a latent form of anger, which doesn't leave visible scars on the intended victim. Sadly, these abusers may sometimes seem like the pillar of the community to those outside of the home. They will often "groom" others into believing they are the one being taken advantage of by their partner or spouse. This leaves the real victim with no one to believe them if they gathered up the nerve to tell

Martial Hearts

someone. Don't believe the lie that you deserved it. You are a beautiful child of God and deserve to be loved as Jesus loved, as Mohammed loved, etc.

There can be hope for these situations. But the best defense is prevention. Knowledge is power, and knowing this can help you stand up for yourself before you are taken hostage in such a relationship (which, remember, starts off with only warning signs and not full-blown abuse). Don't rush into the relationship. Take it slow like I've said over and over. Take it slow!

Make a list below of abuse warning signs you have seen in yourself and others:

_____

_____

_____

_____

_____

Some people believe they can change or save the other person. This is a dangerous and often disastrous delusion. There is no such thing as missional dating. If you are the one who is experiencing uncontrollable anger, there is help available when you decide you are willing to reach out for it and change your life for the better. Asking trustworthy adults for direction is a good way to get started.

Examples of anger in relationship are grabbing, hitting, abusive sex, aggressive language, yelling, force, refusal to accept no, and connecting sex with power.

Contributions to this type of behavior can be found in role models, music videos, music lyrics, television shows, movies, and sometimes in the family unit itself (father, mother, brother, uncle). Not watching movies or listening to music that promote violence against women and/or society as a whole is the best way to prevent the brain from accepting this action as being normal or acceptable. Thought develops into actions, which develop into character, which forms our lifestyle.

Write some role-modeled anger traits, which come to mind from the examples mentioned above or others or even yourself.

_____

_____

_____

_____

Preventative Listening Skills (Red Flags)

Listen to what people say and watch their related actions. If they become irritated over small things (even if it is not directed toward a person), it's a warning sign. Watch for violent language, such as referring to a person as *that* as in "I want a piece of that!" or by using expressions, which have a violent nature, such as "I would just kick the door in." We can kid ourselves into believing such terms have become common expressions, but people who are able to be involved in a positive, healthy relationship will not be using these expressions. Think about that!

What do we do if we feel this may be happening to us? By now, I think you know my recommendation. Talk to someone! I would recommend asking a professional for direction. Check your phone book or Google for local abuse and protection programs. These programs were developed because of this type of behavior, and these professionals know the ins and outs of helping you without making it public knowledge. Many of them were abused themselves. If you end up leaving and you have a car, be sure it doesn't have OnStar turned on. If it does, the car's location can be tracked. There are also Web sites and eight hundred numbers listed in the front of this book for you or a friend who needs to ask questions. Just call them and ask; you don't have to make a commitment. If your phone is monitored for numbers called, use a friend's phone.

Write down the names of people you would trust talking to if you had such a problem. Include contact information for quick referral.

_____
_____
_____
_____
_____

How can youth prevent development of rage within themselves as they grow older? Start with only saying nice things. Don't belittle or call people names, such as stupid. Don't tell people to shut up. Learn to accept the different opinions of others by practicing the skills taught in this workbook.

If you experience anger toward people you can't seem to control, try this: picture that person walking around Walmart, wearing nothing but a diaper. It's difficult to hang onto your anger when you're laughing hysterically.

Accusations

An *unfounded* accusation is not an emotion but rather an action for creating false or exaggerated statements to frighten, threaten, and ultimately control the intended target. Accusations can be used to take the focus away from the actions of the abuser and place it on an unsuspecting and innocent victim.

For example: your girlfriend or boyfriend says they are going to stay home on Friday and study. Then you find out they were out all night at a party. When you ask them about it, they become outraged at your lack of trust. They blame you for being untrustworthy, thereby removing and redirecting the focus from their own actions onto your actions. They become the victim, and you are to blame. You find yourself on the defensive. Don't let them off the hook. Stick to the original question.

As with insecurity, accusations can also be a way of manipulating an existing insecurity in the target in order to create a defensive position, where the victim feels they need to make it up to the controller. For example, they may make you think you've hurt their feelings, causing you to feel sorry for them for what you did, even though you really didn't do anything. Sexual cons may use this as a way of getting their target to have sex as a form of making up or proving devotion. If there is one phrase I believe needs to be repeated over and over to all people, it is this: *Sex doesn't mean love, and love doesn't mean sex*. Refer to the section on differences between men and women. By now, you should be recognizing how these behaviors are meant to gain control of other people.

Flattery

Webster's dictionary defines flattery simply as insincere or excessive praise. However, flattery is also a con when it is used as a compliment. *Compliments are specific and sincere, while flattery is vague and misleading*. We may

> Insincere praise often does not address character.

sometimes allow ourselves to accept flattery because it gives us that warm, fuzzy feeling, which makes us feel loved (or just makes us feel good).

An example of a compliment would be, "I really admire how patient you are with your little brother." An example of flattery would be, "Baby, you look hot in that bikini" or

"Hey, your car would look hot with me in it." If we base our relationships on looks and possessions, we are being shallow and are not truly looking at a long-term friendship. As I've previously stated, when I was twenty-five years old, I was just out of the Marines and teaching martial arts. I was in good physical shape and pretty cute (so I was told). Now I'm more than twice that age, and I guarantee you, you don't want to see this body in a *Speedo*. If I had been married based on my looks and abilities alone, there would have been no substance to that relationship when the years of life began to wear on my body. Don't get me wrong, there needs to be a physical attraction. But it should not be the only thing you have in common. Also, What if a woman married me because of my possessions or bank account? What would she have done when the cancer wiped us out financially?

Insincere praise often does not address character. Although a con artist may know how to manipulate a compliment, the warning signs will most likely show up shortly in their behavior. Remember, they want a quick relationship. Excessive praise would be when a true compliment is given to an extreme. For instance, constantly repeating the same compliment over and over is excessive praise. The phrase "you look nice today" is a compliment, but if it is repeated constantly, be careful. It could be someone who is shy and wants to speak to you, but just doesn't know how. Or it could be a con from someone who wants to quickly gain your trust by flattering you.

Confronting the person by asking them why they often repeat the statement may give you some insight. If the person begins to blush and withdraw, they may just be insecure and don't know how to talk to someone they think is awesome. If the person dismisses it with no regard, they may not be insecure at all and could have come up with other dialogue, rather than constantly referring to your manner of dress. Angry denial or blaming you for not accepting a simple compliment pretty much exposes the con being caught with his hand in the cookie jar. List some examples of flattery from your own experience. Something someone told you, or you told them, or you heard it happen to someone else. Don't be ashamed. We've all done it.

Status

Status in the community or in school can lead to bullying and intimidation in order to maintain a sense of superiority. The popular kids, the church leaders, and other positions of prominence can be very stressful for the person who thinks they need to always present a certain image. Certainly not all persons of authority fit this description; but persons who do fit this description will have a sense of superiority over others. Unfortunately, many youth are just little miniatures of their parents or other "role models."

I once had a martial art school in a small town where I drove to teach classes once a week. Twenty children who were among the first to join the class actually stayed all the way to black belt. However, one of the children failed his first attempt at black belt. His parents were outraged. The mother of the child was a local business owner, and she was most outraged because the daughter of the local lifeguard passed the test on the first try. So a little committee of certain parents set out to let me know which children in town were to receive honors based on their parent's status rather than merit. I didn't give in, and although I lost the rights to the city facility, all of those children absolutely knew they *earned* their belts on merit and not on status. There has not been a successful martial arts class in this small town since.

Another true story in another small town: There was a really sweet family with sons who were handsome and talented athletes, celebrities on the football field and off. They had great dispositions and everyone just loved them. To keep it short, a young lady of adult age had manipulated one of these high school boys into meeting her somewhere, alone. When the mother heard about it, she explained to the boy what was about to happen, and the child made the decision not to allow himself into the trap of a manipulator. Another local mom, big to-do in the church (you know the type,) pushing fifty and still trying to win prom queen, contacted the boy's mother and told her to butt out of her child's social life. Well, after all was said and done, the boys graduated and moved away on college scholarships. The prom queen wannabe was found to be on drugs, and her husband divorced her to preserve his status as a church deacon.

Status in schools, especially high school, can be just as vicious as the adult community. If you want to hang with the popular kids, you may have to dress a certain way, behave a certain way, attend the right functions, and even sever long-time friendships with kids who aren't acceptable to the clique.

Are you popular? If so, list actions that you may look back and see if you could have been a little more accepting of an unpopular student. Are you unpopular? List actions you could take to prevent yourself from being a snob when you grow up and fill out. Not everyone fits in either of these categories, but only you are the one who knows if you do or not.

_____

_____

_____

_____

_____

An example may be the star of the football team or the most popular cheerleader. Certainly, most students in these positions would probably not be this way, but it serves as a good example since schools almost always have a person who stands out among their peers in these capacities. Girls are worse than boys about making their friends behave a certain way, but either may use their status for sex. I once had a student come to me for counseling after his girlfriend (whom he adored) told him she would have sex with him or she would find a new boyfriend who would. I was very proud of the young man for sticking to his morals and preserving the integrity of the most precious gift he could ever give his future wife—his virginity. She dumped him. But that boy is now a happily married man and a wonderful dad.

Students who use status for sex or other behavior may threaten to have their victim (boyfriend or girlfriend) treated harshly by other students for not doing as they are commanded. The threat of a very long and unhappy high school experience is often too much to bear without help. You may see a domineering slave master while the rest of the community sees a hero.

In the adult relationship, it gets even worse. Although you may be reading this and feeling hopeless, there *is* help out there, and you *can* receive it.

One example I like to use in seminars is Spiderguy. Let's suppose that Spiderguy uses his status to control his girlfriend, Webgirl. How would you combat this? Who would listen? The world sees a hero, but in private he has a web spun so tight around his girl that she can't even breathe. The good news is that Spiderguy is not real, and although the abusive relationship may seem that way, and the status abuser may seem to hold all the cards and have all of the power in the community to make your life miserable, help *is* out there.

Bribery

Bribery is defined as any enticement meant to condition behavior. Bribery is often disguised as a gift. However, a gift that requires or has an expectation of something in return is not a gift at all. There are many adults and youth who believe that, for example, if a boy spends a lot of money on a girl when they are on a date, she owes him sex. Girls can often be pressured into doing something against their will because they want to feel loved. A good response for girls who are confronted to pay up for the evening is to offer to go in and let their dad come pay the boy for half of the evening's expense.

Girls can be just as bad, though. I've had several women tell me, after the first book, that women will tell the boy, "You're gonna take me out for a nice time on the town. You ain't gettin' this for free." This is not the behavior of a lady.

Girls can bribe guys with their looks as well. They can easily entice by their manner of dress and body language since boys are stimulated visually. This doesn't mean, however, that every girl who dresses with low bustlines or high hemlines is ringing the chow bell. The desire to be in style and popular attributes greatly to wearing clothes that boys see as come-ons.

There are also girls who believe it is not inappropriate because it's the way other girls dress. I once knew a sweet and beautiful young teenager who was upset because so many boys at school treated her as if she was a whore. Although she didn't display misleading behavior or body language, she didn't know her dress was giving the impression. After all, she told me, it was the same way her mother dressed.

Boys need to learn that every girl who dresses in a way that reveals much of her body is not offering a sexual invitation or, as the old folks used to say, hanging her sign out. But girls need to know that *boys will not treat you like Mother Teresa when you dress like Madonna.*

The most common argument I hear is that "it's hard to find decent clothes." That's true. But if girls would go back to learning how to sew and make their own clothes, the styles in the stores would change. Business people are about money. If your friends start asking you to make clothes for them because they like yours so much, you could pay your way through college with your own business. Necessity is the mother of invention. And, right now, there is an opening for someone who can sew cute clothes for young ladies who wish to dress conservatively.

Control

Control is the ultimate goal of the con. It gives a sense of hopelessness and futility. I've heard of men with so much control over their wives that they will check the odometer on the car to ensure she has not driven one mile more than it takes to drive to work and home.

All of the previously mentioned cons are means of gaining control. The best way to prevent this control is to make relationship building a very long and slow process. If you are trapped in a controlling relationship, remember there is help available. In the front of this book are some Web sites and phone numbers of national organizations created specifically to help people trapped in these situations. You are not alone.

List some experiences where you have yourself tried to control someone. It may have been your little brother or sister, a niece or nephew, your parents or grandparents, a friend or neighbor. Be honest. Don't justify the act with reasons why you did it. List them and do the name-claim-tame activity.

___

___

___

___

___

___

___

___

___

___

18

Teasing

TEASING IS A method a con may use with any of the tactics listed above. You may have noticed people saying, "I was just teasing" after they were confronted or exposed for inappropriate behavior or speech.

Remember that putting thoughts into your head could psychologically break down your defenses. In other words, as we've mentioned before, the more you hear it, the more your brain will accept it.

> Putting thoughts into your head could psychologically break down your defenses.

I knew an adult man who picked a particular young lady as his next target. She was much younger than him. He would call her work and even go by and ask for her. Whoever answered the phone or door, he would say, "Tell her it's her boyfriend." She asked him to not tell people that he was her boyfriend, but he would laugh and say he was just teasing. Well, no he wasn't. He was grooming the other men at her work to understand that she belonged to him. When the "teasing" persisted, she told him to not contact her and stopped spending friendly time with him. It had become clear to her that she was being played. Do you have an example of teasing that you could write out?

_____

_____

_____

_____

_____

_____

See how much you remember about con games by answering these seven fill-in–the-blank statements:

1. A con man is one who quickly gains your confidence and then _____ your trust.
2. The nine listed emotional con games are jealousy and possessiveness, insecurity, intimidation, anger, accusations, flattery, status, bribery, and _____. (The ultimate goal of a con.)
3. The best way to prevent someone from gaining control over you is to make _____ building a slow process.
4. A gift with strings attached is really a _____.

5. _____ in the community or in school can lead to bullying and intimidation in order to maintain a sense of superiority.
6. "I really admire how patient you are with your little brother" is an example of a _____.
7. An example of jealousy and possessiveness is when someone attempts to _____ your relationship.

Answers on page 272.

19

Dating Self-Defense Techniques

ALTHOUGH THESE EXAMPLES are meant to bring insight to ideas on protection for women, books and videos should only be used as a reference to review and remember techniques learned in an atmosphere of hands-on self-defense training through the martial art of your choice.

The majority of self-defense techniques are designed to hurt people. If we could stop assaults by tickling someone or by telling them a joke, then we'd be in the comedy business. But the reality is that it's a big bad world outside, and we need to have a set of tools in which to better claim our right to the pursuit of happiness our forefathers meant for us to enjoy.

The following material used on others for entertainment is crossing the boundaries of others and is abusive behavior.

Although there may be several ways to escape grabs, we will explain

> Four million women a year are assaulted by their partners.

only one. Further into the book, there is a section on how to find an appropriate martial arts school. If the instructor of the school you choose doesn't know these particular moves, don't worry. There are way too many techniques for anyone to know them all. He or she will probably know several techniques of which I am unaware. If, however, they would like to take advantage of my personal knowledge, I am available for seminars and speaking engagements.

Hand on the Leg

The person sitting next to you places his hand on the top or inside of your leg. The hand will most likely be diagonal to sideways on your inner thigh.

Place the blade of your hand on top of the knuckles (from your little finger knuckle to the point finger knuckle).

Grab the hand and pull up on the fingers while pushing down on the knuckles and roll your hand thumb up.

Raise the hand off your leg by bending the fingers back toward the wrist and place it on his own leg. Gently pat the hand a couple of times to let him know he needs to keep his hand on his own leg.

Arm Around the Shoulder

One of the oldest tricks in the book, usually for young insecure boys who are trying to get to "first base" with a girl is to put his arm around her shoulder and then slowly move his hand down toward her breast. There could be any number of reasons why she would allow him to feel her breast.

Some of those reasons are:

- ➢ She wants to feel loved.
- ➢ She thinks everyone does it.
- ➢ She is afraid of losing popularity.
- ➢ She wants to make him happy.
- ➢ She thinks it's owed to him for buying her popcorn.
- ➢ She doesn't want to draw attention by making a scene.
- ➢ She doesn't know how to stop it or how to say no.
- ➢ She thinks it's not a big deal because it's not like going all the way.

The following technique explains the process of using the basics of a wristlock to remove the person's arm from around your shoulder. It causes enough pain to work without insulting the boy's manliness and yet quickly setting a healthy boundary. If the young man respects the boundary, a healthy relationship is being formed. If he rejects it, then this relationship would have ended up one-sided and would not have been healthy. Remember, like the hundred-dollar bill in the beginning of the book, you are highly valued by God and should be treated with all the respect of a princess of His kingdom.

Scenario:

The boy puts his arm around your shoulder and begins moving it down toward your breast.

Defense:

With the hand nearest the boy, reach across to the hand on your shoulder and place your thumb in the middle of his hand.

Grab around his fingers and (keeping your elbow against your body) twist his hand back toward you by pulling your fingers and pushing your thumb.

Next, place your chin on your chest and (again keeping your elbow near your own body) turn slightly toward him and bring his hand around your head.

Finally, turn your shoulders toward him (keep twisting his hand), placing him in a wristlock with his elbow up and his body turning away from you. You may use two hands to reinforce this last move, but remember if too much torque is applied, you could break his wrist. If that happens, it's a pretty safe bet he won't ask you out again.

Be careful not to twist the wrist so much that it breaks. But twist hard enough that he cannot pull out of it. After all, you may want to go out with him again. He just needs to learn to respect your boundaries.

20

Other Self-Defense Moves

How to Hold Your Keys in the Parking Lot

Example one: Our old way of teaching how to hold your car keys for protection in a parking lot was between the fingers. We found two problems with holding the car key in this manner:

1. It was harder to open the car door while holding the keys this way.
2. The key was more difficult to control, often sliding around between the fingers.

Example two: The updated version of how to hold your key for self-defense. Not only do you have better control, but the key can be inserted into the door lock much easier. There are also many other ways to use the key for self-defense.

1. Hold the key in the palm of your hand with your thumb on the head of the key, just as you normally would to open your car door.
2. Hold the hand with the key toward your rear with the other hand in front. This prevents the assailant from grabbing your arm. You can then push the tip of the key into pressure points on the hand if he grabs your lead arm or other places on the body, depending on how he approaches or grabs you.

Another good move to remember is to hold your keys with your hand on the alarm button. You can even use this if someone is trying to get into your apt if you're parked close enough to the door.

Escapes from Grabs

Behind bear hug

Attacker grabs you from behind by wrapping his arms around you just above your elbows, trapping your arms against your body.

Move your hip over to one side, exposing the front lower portion of the attacker's body. Reach high *inside* attacker's leg and pinch and twist the inner thigh. Pinch hard and twist. He lets go; you run away.

Front hug

A person hugs you from the front and either refuses to let go or rubs his body inappropriately against your body.

Place both of your hands on the sides of the aggressor's body just above the beltline and squeeze in a pinching manner with your fingernails into your palms and twist your thumbs in a circular motion toward his back. The most unyielding aggressors become believers when this technique is applied.

Outside wrist grab

Attacker grabs outside of wrist. Move toward attacker rather than away from attacker. Bend arm as if you were striking attacker's arm with your elbow. Pull hand toward the tip of attacker's thumb and twist hand, thumb downward. Keep arm parallel with the ground.

Inside wrist grab

Attacker grabs inside of wrist. Strike the nerve of attacker's arm against the bone with your other hand and pull your grabbed hand toward the tip of attacker's thumb.

Two-hand frontal choke

Attacker grabs throat forcefully pushing you back on to one foot. Swing both hands high into the air. Turn in a circular motion to the direction of the leg which has been forced back.

If attacker has a hold of your throat and is not pushing you back onto one foot, put spear finger into middle of attacker's throat and push tip of fingers into throat while turning sideways and extending arm.

Mounted choke

Attacker has you on the ground with their knees on the ground on both sides of your body and is choking you with both hands.

Bend your knees. Grab attacker's wrist firmly with one hand and place your other hand on their ribs. Buck your hips high into the air (while holding attacker's wrist firmly) and push them sideways with the hand on their ribs.

Roll the opposite way and escape.

Shaking hands

My being a small person, I was so glad to learn how to shake hands without someone squeezing my knuckles. This will prevent an intimidator (unless they're a giant) from squeezing your knuckles. This move must be practiced until it becomes a habit, so get your best friend and practice. Practice everywhere you go by shaking lots of people's hands. By the

> Ninety-three percent of women who killed their mates had been battered by them. Sixty-seven percent killed them to protect themselves and their children at the moment of attempted murder.

way, this is a courtesy, which is a mostly unnoticeable self-defense technique, making it invisible, which some say is the art of the ninja. That's how we got the name: Nice Ninjas.

Place your hand into the other person's hand with your hands firmly together. While holding their fingers with your fingers in the handshake position, extend or relax your point finger. It's as simple as that.

Some cultures bow with their hands in a prayerlike position. They believe touching may transfer negative energy to them. Shaking hands, however, tells you much about the other person. If they squeeze too hard, they are trying to intimidate you. If they are sweating, they are nervous. If their hand is limp, they are passive, etc.

Escaping aggressive handshake

Escaping an aggressive handshake where the other person refuses to let go has many different variations. They range from simply asking the person to let go, to escaping the grasp, to injuring the other person. I will explain only one of several escape techniques. I chose this particular escape because of its similarity to the inside wrist grab. Intimidator shakes hand hard and refuses to let go. Raise left hand up and across your body. Strike radial nerve while pulling right hand free.

Strikes

Palm heel strike

Pull fingers back from open hand and strike (like a punch) with the bottom portion of the hand. The nose is the best target.

Thumb strike

Make vertical fist with thumb laying on side of point finger and extending out past knuckles (wrist straight). Thumb makes an extension of the arm in a straight line. Shove straight into vital area of attacker, such as the eye, hip socket, throat, or pressure point below cheekbone.

Knife hand (karate chop)

Open hand, fingertips bent slightly. Strike with edge of hand in any direction.

Spear hand

Open hand with fingers together and straight. Shove fingernails straight into attacker. Preferably into throat.

Eye slice

Open hand with fingers together and straight. Swing hand, palm down sideways across eyes of attacker, striking with fingernails.

Elbow strike

The elbow can be used for striking areas such as the solar plexus to wind an attacker or the nose to cause pain, bleeding, disorientation, and distraction. To learn, place the tip of your thumb on your chest and strike with the edge of your elbow. You can also strike upward with the side of your elbow to the chin with your palm sliding past your ear over your same side shoulder.

Hammer fist

With hand closed in fist, strike with bottom of hand beneath little finger.

Tiger mouth strike

There are two ways to perform this technique and both are very dangerous. Do not use it for play or in anger. Once used, it cannot be taken back. Self-defense only!

1. Hold hand flat with thumb spread out and fingers together. Strike the throat with the part of your hand between your thumb and point finger.
2. Cup your hand as if you were holding a small glass of water. Strike and grab the Adam's apple of your attacker. Squeeze thumb and fingers together.

21

Finding an Appropriate Martial Arts School

IN READING THIS material, you may understand why martial arts training can be so much more beneficial than just learning how to fight. But finding just the right school for you may take some searching. You may even need to do some traveling to find just the right place. Here are some tips on finding such a place:

1. Don't just send your kids to the most convenient location without investigation. You should be as concerned about who has influence over your child as you are about who cuts your hair.
2. Watch a few classes alone to get a feel for the environment and the attitude of the students and instructors. Your child will emulate them.

3. If students are arrogant, braggarts, or they talk ugly about the other local schools, just leave. The student becomes the instructor.
4. Ask other parents what they like and dislike about the school.
5. Don't worry so much about the style of martial arts as you do the positive or negative atmosphere. There are no bad martial arts, only bad martial artists.
6. Visit several places. Don't select a school based on mysticism or convenience.
7. When you think you've made your choice, speak to the instructor or owner and ask questions. Ask to see credentials. Don't buy the old "my certificate burned up in fire". They can get copies from their international organization headquarters. Ask about all required payments or purchases. Ask about extra costs, such as belt testing. Also remember that belt testing normally increases, so ask about the increase rate and ask what the black belt test costs and what comes with it. You don't usually pay for the belt; you pay for the test. Ask if the belt is awarded or if there is an extra charge.
8. If the school uses contracts (agreements as they are called today), ask if you can take it home and read it. Read it carefully. Don't be pressured into an immediate commitment (even if there is a discount for signing without reading it). You may even wish to consult an attorney if it is too confusing for you.

9. Don't be swept away by a fancy building if there is no substance to the teaching. You may or may not recognize poor instruction, but you should be able to see good or poor character. Which of these three options do you want mentoring your child into the adult they will become?
   a. Do you want a cheap karate day care with no discipline?
   b. Do you want your child to learn fear through harsh, boot-camp training?
   c. Do you want your child to learn respect from proper role modeling, and discipline through a structured, nourishing environment?
10. If you choose a school with a contract, you may wish to write an option to stop attending without penalty if the environment becomes threatening, has a poor role model working with students, or becomes sexually harassing. Have the owner's initial next to your line. Remember, contracts build trust. They should protect you as a consumer and not just protect the seller.

If you are enrolling a child, they really do need to learn to make a commitment and not just quit everything they start because it becomes too hard (see "Who's in Charge"). Don't freak out if they get a little bruise. This is martial arts. It is designed to save your life. Children who are allowed to constantly quit activities may have serious difficulty staying with a job or a marriage when one or both of them become difficult, and they will.

It's a tough job for martial art instructors to know their budget when students just up and quit without meeting their financial obligations. Many instructors must work a full-time day job and teach at night just to survive. They do it because they love it and because they care about your safety and that of your children. They deserve to be able to depend on you.

If you prefer, ask for a short-term contract, like three months or six months rather, than a year or longer. It may cost a little more, but if you decide to stick with it, then you can get a cheaper rate for a longer period of time.

11. If you sign up a child, let the teacher be the teacher. Don't yell out instructions from the bleachers. That's not your job. It may even cause your child to want to quit because it's not their own personal activity. Take pictures and make scrapbooks with your child. Praise your child for their effort and never tell them they aren't good enough. The instructor will help them improve over time. Let him or her do the job which they have spent years perfecting. One of my best black belts failed his brown belt test 4 times. That's every test for a solid year. He had to work hard for everything he "earned".

12. Don't become your child's instructor and teach them at home by slapping them around in order to make them tough. You won't make them tough; you'll make them afraid. Let a trained professional work with your child, and you just enjoy watching them have fun. Your job is to encourage and support. Love them as much when they fail as you do when they succeed. Let them build character. This is most difficult for parents who coach a sport and feel they must always win.
13. Never, by any means, compare your child with another to the instructor. You don't know (and they won't tell you) any special situations other children are dealing with away from class. If you expect special treatment because of your status in the community, you may be surprised when your child's karate teacher isn't easily intimidated.
14. Don't listen to others (even friends) who tell you horrible things about your child's instructor. Horrible things they were told at a competing martial art school. You've made your choice based on probably more thorough investigation than the rumor spreader. You may need to stand up to the peer pressure of your friends if you want your children to stand up to the peer pressure of their friends. Children learn by example.

I strongly recommend martial art training. It doesn't need a season or a day of sunshine. You don't need to be pretty, slim, or athletic. You can practice with a team, by yourself, or with your entire family. You can be competitive or just stay fit. Because of the discipline, confidence and respect developed. If you practiced self-defense your entire life and were never attacked, the time would not have been wasted.

22

Stories

THE FOLLOWING PAGES are stories I wish to share with you. Not because I wrote them to be held in esteem by man. Rather, because I wrote them to inspire and encourage others. Some of these stories are examples of traits learned in this *Martial Hearts* book. Look for the morals. I hope you enjoy them.

The following paragraph introduces the first story.

Many people bring their families to my self-defense school not as much for the physical training as they do for the emotional benefits. Brokenheartedness seems to be a growing epidemic in our country. It's no wonder with all the divorced, single parent, learning-disabled families. As parents pour out their heart to me, I am often reminded of a story. I call it,

Danny Passmore

The Harp

"Many, many years ago, on a cold wintry evening, a homeless vagrant knocked on the door of a modest suburban home. An elderly lady opened the door as the man spoke in a shivering voice, 'Lady, you don't know me from Adam, and I won't blame you if you shut the door in my face right now, but I must tell you, if I spend one more night in this freezing cold, I surely will die.'

'Don't say another word,' answered the homeowner. 'You just come right inside here, and I'll fix you a little place in the basement.' She led her guest to the basement where he immediately noticed a harp over in the corner of his lower level sanctuary. 'Why do you have your beautiful harp down here?' he asked.

The woman explained how that harp had belonged to her late husband. 'Many a night, he would play such beautiful music for me on that harp. Then he passed away, and as I moved out here to the suburbs, into a smaller house, the moving company dropped and broke my treasured harp. Naturally, they offered to have it fixed, but no one in the entire state does harp repair. So there it sits.' She sighed, wiped a small tear from her eye, and then regained her composure as she said, 'Now, you just settle in down here, and I'll go upstairs and fix you a nice warm bowl of soup.'

Later that evening, the lady heard the most beautiful music coming from the basement. She rushed downstairs to find this raggedly dressed bum playing beautifully on her now-repaired harp. She stared in disbelief as the man stopped, and seeing the puzzled look on her face, began to answer her look. 'I haven't always been a bum, ma'am,' the man said. 'You see, before the depression bankrupted me, I owned my own business.' He continued, 'I made harps. In fact, I made this harp, and once you've made something, you can always mend it.'"

The moral of the story is this: no matter what tragedies we may face in our lives, the one who made our hearts can mend our hearts.

Our society has ousted God and made Him homeless in our lives. But He's still out there knocking, waiting to see who is going to open the door and invite Him in.

Special Needs

As I tied the fourth-degree black belt around her waist, I reflected back to when Josie was a little girl with a big problem.

Although she is a very patient and mild-mannered young lady now, as a child she had one of the most volatile tempers I have ever seen.

It seemed that anything would set her off and then she was fists, feet, and elbows all over the person closest to her. But with a little compassion and a lot of patience, Josie overcame her anger problem and went on to master the art of tae kwon do.

Josie's story is just one of hundreds in which a special need was tended to, and a once insecure child developed into a successful and happy young adult.

There have been many "special needs" students at my martial arts school. I have taught students who were blind, deaf, ADD, LD, crippled, cerebral palsy sufferers, autistic, and many more.

Anytime someone asks me how it is that I can work so well with these individuals, I like to share this little story with them:

> A young boy was walking down a street in his neighborhood when he saw a sign which read, "Puppies for Sale." The boy hurried up to the front door of the house, knocking excitedly in hopes of getting a new pet. As a man answered the door, a flood of puppies poured out the door and surrounded the boy, jumping and yelping for their share of attention.
>
> "How much for one of these puppies?" asked the youngster. The owner explained how these were hunting dogs and cost two hundred dollars each. "Do you have two hundred dollars?" asked the man.
>
> The boy put on his best business face and dug deep into his pocket, eventually pulling out six pennies and a marble.
>
> As the dog owner tried to think of a way to gently let the boy down, another member of the litter showed up.

The last pup, with a crippled leg, had finally made his way to the door for his share of loving from the young lad. When the boy saw the pup struggling along on his bad leg, the boy's eyes grew large as saucers as he exclaimed loudly, "Oh, mister, I want *that* dog."

The man explained how this dog was no good as a hunting dog and was soon to be put out of his misery. "I'll tell you what," said the man. "I'll let you have this dog if you can tell me why it is you prefer this old crippled dog rather than a healthy one." The boy reached down and pulled up his pant leg and there, from the knee to the ankle, was a brace. The boy said, "Because he needs someone who understands him."

We may not all wear leg braces or sit in wheelchairs. We may not all use white canes or wear hearing aids. But we all have our special needs, and we need people in our lives who understand us. So what's my special need? Well, that's another story.

For the previous story, I first heard it told in an "open" meeting of Alcoholics Anonymous. An open meeting means anyone is welcome to attend (student, clergy, concerned family member, etc.) as opposed to a "closed" meeting, which is reserved only for persons with a desire to stop drinking.

I later learned it was a version of the story told in Jack Canfield's book *Chicken Soup for the Soul*. I modified it somewhat.

Danny Passmore

The White Suit Story

In the late '70s, I bought a three-piece white suit. It was a nice suit, and I liked to wear it with a soft blue shirt and a blue tie with black patent leather shoes. Once I quit drinking, however, I suddenly became very self-conscious and feared wearing the suit as it was somewhat conspicuous.

I was working at a furniture store in Austin, Texas, when the owner threw a party for the employees at a fancy restaurant. I dressed up in my white suit and drove down to the restaurant. When I arrived, I was surprised that I couldn't get out of the car. I was in so much fear of walking in wearing this suit that I couldn't even open the car door. It was an elegant restaurant, and my dress was appropriate for the dinner, but that didn't seem to matter. I was just plain scared. So I drove back home, got undressed, and went to bed.

The next day, I confided in a friend about what had just happened. He suggested I wear the suit to work since I worked in the office where a coat and tie was required. So I hung my suit on the doorknob of the closet (so I wouldn't "forget" to wear it.) Then I went to bed, but I couldn't sleep. I was so worried about the next day that my eyes wouldn't shut. Finally, I got up in the middle of the night and put the suit on. Here I was, at 2:00 a.m., standing in front of the bathroom mirror fully clothed, tie, shoes, the whole works. I remember looking at myself and saying out loud, "There is nothing wrong with this suit!" So why was I so afraid to wear it?

The next morning, I got up and left for work about forty-five minutes early so I would have time to chicken out and go back home to change. Since I arrived early, I went into the break room where the salesmen were having coffee and getting ready for their day. Everyone looked up as I held my breath. Then they returned to their conversations. Now I'm mad. I went through all of this and there was not even a giggle. Nothing! Then one of the ladies told me I looked nice. Was this all? I thought for sure I would be laughed out of the store.

I like to tell this story because it describes how fear can literally paralyze us without cause. If we face our fears and walk through the situation with blind faith, we may often see the fear was unjustified. It was a **F**alse **E**vent **A**ppearing **R**eal. That's all. You can have faith and fear at the same time. It's called courage. The next time you find yourself fearing something, I hope you will remember my white suit story.

My Greatest Christmas Gift

For the last two years, my family didn't have much of a chance to really celebrate Christmas. I was fighting for my life. Cancer had ravaged my body with massive tumors in my spleen, pancreas, and intestines. I watched the attack on America at the trade towers from my hospital deathbed with our pastor standing on one side of my bed and my wife standing on the other. The doctors kept me free from pain as they waited for death to arrive, but I survived.

I waited for my business to go under as I lay helpless in bed for months, but it survived. I worried about the pressure on my new marriage of only a year. That, too, survived.

I marveled at the timing of my new insurance becoming active, which covered much of the treatment costs. Yet, I regretted beginning the building of my dream home just before the illness struck.

I had no control over what would happen next. I could accept death if it was to be because the last fifteen years of my life had been dedicated to helping others. But my wife fervently prayed for God not to take the love of her life so quickly in our relationship. I fought, and people prayed hard.

Cards and money poured in from family, friends, church members, and the community. An international martial arts magazine, which sometimes covered my school, printed my situation. Phone calls and letters of support came in from across the country. The boost to my morale was tremendous. I felt like Jimmy Stewart in *It's a Wonderful Life* being allowed to see how many lives I had touched.

This year, after several near-death encounters as well as several operations, I am cancer-free. Rather than shrivel, my business thrived. My marriage is strong and secure as we enjoy the comfort and space of our new home.

Positive attitude, prayer, and radical medical treatment saved me. But now comes the really good news. After being on death row (as it were) and getting a last-minute reprieve, I find myself enjoying the greatest gift I could ever receive for Christmas.

Somehow, over the years, I seemed to have forgotten what it means to be touched by grace. I've been given this wonderful opportunity to understand what issues are most important in life. God had pruned back my branches so I could blossom.

I can get upset about divisive politics that contradict the flag waving and unity this country needs. I can steam over dishonest business people and individuals who rob the innocent through fraud and deceit.

I can really blow my top over the promotion of immoral and un-Christian agendas. But no longer do I allow those issues to control me.

The greatest gift I've ever received is in knowing that I am powerless. It was God who handled the big decision of allowing me to live a little longer on this earth. I believe He'll handle these little things in life as well. Thank you, God, for this wonderful Christmas gift. And happy birthday, Jesus.

The Fighting Wolves

There was a medicine man in the Huaco Indian tribe in Texas who would occasionally counsel young braves. One day, his son questioned him on a story he overheard his father tell a brave with problems of angry outbursts. "My father," said the boy. "You told this brave each of us have two wolves inside of us. A good wolf and a bad wolf, fighting against each other. You said his quick outbursts of anger without thinking causes the bad wolf inside of him to win, and that he must learn to let only the good wolf win the battle."

"Yes, my son. Do you have a question about these wolves inside each of us?" replied the wise old medicine man.

"Yes, father" answered the boy. "I have watched your actions many years. How is it that your good wolf always wins?"

"Ah," answered the father. "Because, that is the wolf I feed."

Unending Hurt of Drug Abuse

I am hurting. I am again suffering the effects of drug abuse. My friend is dying, and I am powerless to help. I cannot force her to stop, nor can I let her take me with her. I can only love her, pray for her, and try not to enable her.

Several years ago, I met her at a place where people learn to recover from a seemingly hopeless state of mind and body. I was one of those who helped this lady sober up. Again. The last time we spoke was just before she overdosed.

My friend had a drug problem, but the drugs were only a symptom of her disease. Like so many, she used drugs and alcohol to cover her feelings, her guilt, her loneliness, and her despair. These feelings are brought on by the problem, which was the root of her illness: my friend lies.

Only the alcoholic can empathize with the obsession created after just one drink of alcohol. Only the overeater can empathize with the obsession after one bite of sugar. But only God can restore us to sanity from the problems that drive us to our addictions.

This isn't the first time I've witnessed the seriousness of alcoholism and drug abuse. Four years ago, I buried a friend whom I had met through martial arts in the 1970s. All of my friend's karate experience could not help him when he chose to stick that needle in his arm. I suffered heavily during that time from my friend's drug abuse.

Three years ago, a fellow high school graduate put a gun in his mouth and pulled the trigger. He could accept no other alternative to deal with his problems. I suffered from drug abuse.

Two years ago, I watched a friend drink himself to death. Again, I suffered from drug abuse.

Last year, a fellow martial artist was involved in an alcohol-related car accident, which claimed the lives of several people. Again, I, and many others, suffered from drug abuse.

Now, this year, my very dear friend is in intensive care. Again, I am suffering from the disease of alcoholism and drugs. I am no longer as bitter against those who sell, use, and condone drug usage, except for those in my profession who are such poor role models.

In spite of my years of sobriety, I find that every time I deal with one resentment, fear, or character flaw, another one crops up. For me, drug and alcohol abuse are a daily battle, but I must continue the fight.

How do I fight this battle? I have dedicated my life to my Master who set me, a disabled veteran, free from the darkness of alcohol and drug abuse. I will continue to teach others that self-defense is an inside job. I will continue to stress that the only true Master of our lives is God.

To lie, cheat, steal, disrespect authority, and reject education is the road to drugs, jail, and death. I will continue to be the best role model I can be and encourage other adults to be good role models as well. I will not give up on others because my greatest role model and savior never gave up on me.

Texas Teen Hears Tae Kwon Do's Call

(*Tae Kwon Do Times* Magazine, May 1998)

At age fourteen, Bryan Goines has already reached more goals than most adults achieve in a lifetime. He has certified black belts with the World Taekwondo Federation (TKD), the World Tangsoodo Association (TSD) and an international Hapkido Federation. In addition to teaching classes at the school that he and his father own, Brian is adding to his martial arts prowess by studying American Jujitsu and wrestling. Bryan is also deaf.

As a small child attending school in Waco, Texas, deaf children were not educated at the same level as hearing children. For this reason, as well as other factors, Bryan severely withdrew from the outside world. His devoted parents, Charles and Mary Goines, sought any help in rearing a deaf child to live a normal life in a hearing world.

Although a professional counselor had advised the Goines not to allow their child to learn sign language (a surprisingly common attitude in the US), Charles and Mary decided to learn his language (American sign language, ASL) and then teach him their languages (English and Spanish).

Charles was also very concerned about how little Bryan often clung to his father's pant leg in public and would go out of his way to avoid other children. In order to boost the self-confidence of his son, Mr. Goines decided to enroll his son in a local Korean Taekwondo school. It didn't help.

Bryan's initial enthusiasm for martial arts quickly faded, and he would cry when his mother insisted that he get ready for class. Even though parents were not allowed to observe classes, the Goines soon learned why the boy was so upset. The instructor, who barely could speak English, would not allow Bryan to participate in the class and would instead send the boy to sit out of the way while the other children practiced.

Charles then decided to enroll in a martial arts class in Huntsville where he commuted to work daily. He chose a Tang Soo Do dojang under Master Allen Sharpe and set a goal to get his black belt and teach Bryan himself.

Danny Passmore

Charles and Mary told Bryan of their new plans. Instead of being excited, the child was devastated. Due to his own negative experience with the martial arts, he considered all martial arts to be bad and didn't want his father participating. Then came the big break that changed the Goine's lives.

Mary heard a friend talking about Danny Passmore, a local American who taught tae kwon do and was also an interpreter for the deaf. It almost seemed too good to be true, but Mary discussed this new information with her husband, and the two decided this time they should check the credentials of the instructor.

Through their research, the Goines found that Mr. Passmore was a certified tae kwon do instructor (the same rank as the local Korean instructor and through the same Kukkiwon organization located in Seoul, Korea). Not only that, but he was a college degreed ASL interpreter for the deaf. And people who knew of him said he was a highly respected role model and a Christian. Feeling confident this would not be like his previous experience, they took Bryan to observe a class.

Also unlike his prior dojang, spectators were welcome and parents were encouraged to come view classes. The boy's little eyes lit up like Christmas when he saw that classes were taught in voice and sign. He searched the class for students wearing hearing aids. "One, two, three," he counted. *Oh my goodness*, little Bryan thought to himself. *Almost all of the students were deaf or hard of hearing.*

Martial Hearts

After class, the instructor and students introduced themselves to the visitors and briefly chatted with parents and spouses. They all formed an immediate bond with Bryan as he was the only deaf child; the others were all college students. That bond is still true today.

Bryan became a regular in the class. He learned all of the positive aspects of true martial arts in his own language. He immediately began to come out of his shell revealing a young man who was jovial, intelligent, and considerate of others. No longer did he cling to his father's pant leg and hide his face from other children. In fact, he would always help hearing children learn to feel comfortable around him at tae kwon do tournaments and other hearing functions. Where he once would cry if he had to go to class, now he cried if he couldn't go to class.

The elder Goines also continued his Tang Soo Do training, and father and son achieved black belt in their respective styles at about the same time. Also during this period, Charles resigned from his job in TV repair at the state prison and opened his own TV and VCR repair shop in Waco so that he could have more time to enjoy his family.

Charles and Bryan opened their own Tang Soo Do school in the back room of the TV shop and soon had several students. Bryan also continued his tae kwon do study as the father-son team both achieved second degree and began to train each other in their respective styles.

About a year later, Charles was offered another position with the prison where he had previously worked, with a raise and benefits good enough to merit serious consideration. Since the family was still disappointed with the Waco School District's policies toward educating the deaf, they did some investigating into the education of deaf children in the Huntsville-Bryan-College Station area.

Impressed with their finding, they asked their friend, Danny Passmore, for advice about what to do with their school. They certainly didn't want to just walk away from the dedicated students, even if it was only a few. Passmore offered to allow a Saturday morning class and let the Goines use his facility on weekends, which would be a two-and-one-half-hour drive one way to teach their Waco students.

The Goines enrolled Bryan in the deaf education program in the town, which coincidentally had the same name as their son, Bryan. Now attending Tang Soo Do class during the week with his father, Bryan received a black belt in that system. Charles, learning from his son, tested under Mr. Passmore, and became a black belt in tae kwon do.

The Tang Soo Do master, Allen Sharpe, and the tae kwon do master, Danny Passmore, became friends and both joined a growing Hapkido federation. Bryan would then go on to receive a black belt in Hapkido, as well as his third degree in TKD.

In 1997, Bryan received his first major award when he was inducted into the Texas Martial Arts Hall of Fame for outstanding achievement.

Bryan then joined the Bryan wrestling team and performed spectacularly. His academic educators worked with Bryan's speech to improve his communication skills. He became able to speak to hearing people and was a prolific lip-reader.

His mom says now that Bryan spends a lot of time lifting weights and combing his hair in the bathroom until he gets his hair just right. "He's just a typical, normal teenage boy," says his mother. "Just like we always wanted."

My Last Rodeo

It was a typical spring day. The sun was out with the hint of a cool breeze hanging over from winter. I had just met Jacob at the karate school. He was buying me out since I was retiring. The injuries I sustained during my service in the marines had progressed to the point where I couldn't even just be there while other black belts taught. So I was teaching Jacob the business part during this transition.

As we were in the office, in through the door walked six police officers, three of them with Taser in their hands. What now, I wondered. *More harassment from that crazy woman next door?* I wondered. I would soon find out it was much worse. I told Jacob to call my wife as they handcuffed my wrists and ankles. I guess they thought I was going to go Bruce Lee on them.

When the detective put me in the car, he told me I was being arrested for abusing a child in my karate class. "What?

Who!" The child I was asked to mentor by the local office of Mental Health and Mental Retardation (MHMR) a year and a half ago had told his counselor that I did the same things his dad had done to him. I was in shock! I knew he was upset because I was retiring, and he might need a new mentor. *Was he confused or angry?* I thought to myself, *Was he joking? There had to be a reason.* I thought maybe he was trying to prevent me from leaving. Maybe this was his way to deal with rejection. But we had talked about my disabilities, and he understood and was very supportive with my retiring due to my health. At least I thought he was.

"So are you going to talk to us?" asked the detective. *What should I do?* I wondered. If I tell them where I was on any particular day or time, they'll just change it until they find a day or time for which I had no alibi. I've seen them do it before. "If I talk to you, will I still go to jail?" I asked the detective. This is the same detective who made up a story for the woman next door and arrested me for a day. But this was different. He said we'd go to jail either way, so I just told him to take me on to jail. They put me in protective custody in the county jail while I sweated out the medications the Veterans Administration (VA) had me on for my disabilities and other ailments.

Then I saw the judge, and he set the bond at a quarter-of-a-million dollars. This was just getting more and more bizarre. It took me three days in bed to sweat out all of the medication my doctor had me taking. Diabetes, pain, depression due to the pain, blood pressure, neuropathy, not to mention my disabilities. On the fourth day, I was able to get up and eat something. Then I started meeting the other men.

I watched the news when the anchor, my friend and member of my board of directors, spun the accusation to sound as guilty as possible. I would find out later how one station put on their Web site the doctor who examined the child said there was evidence of tearing in the child's rectum. They didn't report, however, the doctor said it had happened several years ago and was completely healed. No wonder why people who didn't know me thought it was for real.

With my second book on my mind, I started asking the men what type of relationship they had with their fathers. Only one out of twenty had a healthy relationship with his dad. That was a good statistic to show how kids can turn out with no positive male influence in their life. Since Juju was my cell neighbor, I was able to have long talks with him about faith. And not just the talking, but he would later say he learned more by watching the way I interacted with the other inmates. If I had to be there, I was going to spend the time as Jesus would. Juju received thirty years in prison for aggravated armed robbery, which he committed so he could buy twenty dollars' worth of drugs, and we still stay in touch by mail.

My lawyer worked hard for me. He reminded the district attorney of our Constitution that they had ninety days to either indict or release. Since there was never any evidence of wrong behavior, of course, I felt sure they would be forced to release me.

Surprisingly to me, I didn't feel any resentment toward any of the parties involved. An incident was reported. The police had to be notified, and they always arrest first and talk later. The media are all upstanding citizens who love their kids and serve in their church. But when they get together at work, they seek out a life they can destroy to get those ratings up or those newspapers sold. What a surprise to me that I felt no anger. The only thing that bothered me was those few people who thought I could perform such a horrible act on another human being, and especially a child. *That* is what broke my heart.

So, three months later, on the ninetieth afternoon, I was released from jail. There was no mention of innocence in the media. In fact, the local paper said I might still be arrested again. There had been no pornography on my computer nor on videotapes or in books laying around the house. No dirt to dig up. There was none to dig up. I had been touched by grace long before now, and I live only for Christ. Sure, I'm not perfect, but that's the very reason He sacrificed Himself for me. But this hurt me.

It took a lot of counseling, but after four years, God healed me. I still pray for all those involved. That's the best way to help someone. I believe that. So, now, I live near the beach, and I tour the country on my Harley. I was puzzled for a long time as to what God wanted me to do. I lost interest in martial arts or working with children, but what does he want me to do now? On one of my long-distance trips, as I rode down a scenic road, He spoke to my heart and said, "Danny, you don't always need to be Martha. It's okay to be Mary for a while. Just enjoy being with me." And *I am*.

What Experience Has Taught Me

- You don't have to be tall to be a big person.
- Sometimes when you win, you lose; and sometimes when you lose, you win.
- Bad things don't happen to us. They happen for us.
- Never put anything in writing what you wouldn't want read aloud in public.
- Our lives can change with every breath we take.
- A half-truth is still a whole lie.
- All sunshine makes a desert.
- I'm grateful God gives me mercy rather than justice.
- God will use our character defects to help others grow, and vice versa.
- Be careful what you pray for, you might get it.
- The sun shines on the just and the unjust.
- People are not thieves because they steal. They steal because they are thieves.
- If my only tool is a hammer, every problem is a nail.
- You can't walk hand in hand with someone going in a different direction.

- What we do in life echoes in eternity.
- Trust Allah, but tie up your camel.
- No matter where you go, there you are.
- The greater the tragedy, the greater the blessing, if you stay on the right path.
- If you're not the lead elephant, the view is always the same.
- When God closes one door, he opens another. But it's hell in the hallway.
- When you drink from the water, you must remember the spring.
- To go fast, you must go alone; but to go far, you must go together.
- It is better to humble yourself before others than to be humbled by them.
- We are known for our actions, not our intentions.
- There is no winner in a fight.
- When searching for God, the first thing to know is He isn't the one lost.
- If you believe yourself to be humble, you're not.
- Happiness is an illusion propagated by luxury.
- If you want to know a person's heart, look in their check register.
- If no one else has done such a bad deed as you, why is there a name for it?
- My life is none of my business.

- The same raindrop, which denies causing the flood, will take credit for ending the drought.
- There is a big difference between giving up and letting go.
- There is no spoon.
- You can't give away what you ain't got.
- Don't believe everything you think.
- Happiness isn't getting what you want; it's accepting what you get.
- The storms of life are never in the forecast.
- The people who matter don't mind the little things, and the people who mind the little things don't matter.
- God will use our imperfect nature to work His perfect will.
- Two ding-a-lings don't make a bell.
- It's better to be a bird than a turtle.
- Sometimes we need to take the cotton from your ears and put it in our mouth.
- Do you want to be happy, or do you want to be right?
- Everyone has life, but few really know how to live it.
- Don't believe everything you think.
- Every decision has either a result or a consequence.
- You may be the only Bible some people will ever read.
- Self-will blocks the entry of God into my life.
- A tranquil mind is the first requisite for good judgment.
- Peace of mind cannot be bought at the expense of others.

- Self-pity is a common symptom of emotional insecurity.
- Fear is the chief activator of character defects.
- Acceptance is the key to all my problems.
- A healthy relationship with my Creator is like an oasis in the desert of futility.
- Facing death is hard, but facing life is harder.
- Don't get your self-esteem at the expense of others.
- He who conquers himself is greater than he who conquers a city.
- It's hard to remember your main mission was to drain the swamp when you're up to your ass in alligators.

What Experience Has Taught Me Explained

Caution: These are personal interpretations from the author and contains mention of God.

1. **You don't have to be tall to be a big person**
    a. I was always insecure about being short. I once purchased lifts, which I put in the heel of my shoes to add an inch or so to my height. My big brother told me this quote, but he taught me by his example that God measures me by my heart, not my height.
2. **Sometimes when you win, you lose; and sometimes when you lose, you win.**

a. If you win a karate trophy because you lied about your age and/or your level of experience, well, you know inside you're not a winner.
   b. If you let a friend or sibling beat you in a game to build their self-esteem, you are definitely a winner in my book.
3. **Bad things don't happen to us; they happen for us.**
   a. Character is forged in the fire of adversity.
   b. The problem in life is not the bad things that happen; the problem is how we accept and deal with the reality of the situation.
4. **Never put anything in writing that you wouldn't want read aloud in public.**
   a. This was true in my day because it could be kept and later shown to others. But today's youth are putting things on the Internet, which they will deeply regret when they are older and get a job at a respectable firm, or feel a calling to ministry, or decide to run for a political office or have children.
5. **Our lives can change with every breath we take.**
   a. You can sunbathe on the deck of your boat one morning and be dashed on the rocks in that same afternoon.
6. **A half-truth is still a whole lie.**
   a. If you believe there is such a thing as a white lie, you are living in darkness. Step into the sunshine of the spirit where the truth will set you free.

7. **All sunshine makes a desert.**
    a. There is an old saying, "If you want to ruin a man, give him 40 years of prosperity." Then he won't need you, and he won't need God. Children who never fail have trouble accepting problems later in life.
    b. Marriage will be less than getting your way all of the time. You may apply for a job and not be hired. Those who are accustomed to success without failure may, at one point in life, consider suicide because they never learned to accept defeat.
8. **I'm grateful God gives me mercy rather than justice.**
    a. I think we can all understand the meaning of this sentence.
9. **God will use our character defects to help others grow, and vice versa.**
    a. I have turned my life over to God, yet I struggle with gossip. And you have turned your life over to God, yet you struggle with lies. Should you not owe me gratitude rather than anger when I tell someone you lied to them? You may need to think about this one for a while.
10. **Be careful what you pray for, you might get it.**
    a. I knew an impatient, out-of-work girl who prayed for patience and got a job driving a school bus.
11. **The sun shines on the just and the unjust.**
    a. I used to wonder why bad people would profit in this world. Truthfully, for me, it's better when I

stop judging God because of what appears to be success in bad people. The truth may be that they are deeply unhappy with life although the outside looks like they have everything you could want. It's only important for me to focus on me and my honest relationship with my Creator.

12. **People are not thieves because they steal; they steal because they are thieves.**
    a. A person's heart will command his actions.
13. **If your only tool is a hammer, every problem is a nail.**
    a. To solve the most serious and hurtful problems in life, we must arm ourselves with the tools of forgiveness, charity, and love.
14. **You can't walk hand in hand with someone going in a different direction.**
    a. There is a big difference between helping someone change for the better when they've made a bad choice, and someone who continuously and deliberately chooses bad choices over and over and over again.
15. **What we do in life echoes in eternity.**
    a. People say you can't take it with you when you go, but that's not true. According to people who have had near-death experiences, the two things you can take with you are love and knowledge.
    b. I believe what love we have shown in life will determine where we sit at the table before the

throne. True love is from the heart with pure motives for the benefit of the person, the people, and the kingdom.

16. **Trust Allah, but tie up your camel.**
    a. Although we trust God that what He does is for our own benefit, we still need to use our common sense to do the next right thing.
17. **No matter where you go, there you are.**
    a. You can't run away from your problems when the problem is you.
18. **The greater the tragedy, the greater the blessing.**
    a. My personal experience has been that for every tragedy I faced with faith and love, the blessing has either met or exceeded the degree of that tragedy. One took several years, but I knew God would be faithful.
19. **If you're not the lead elephant, the view is always the same.**
    a. Although this statement is graphic, it quickly gets its message across. Some people need to live within a box. They know how much each check from work will bring in and budget accordingly. And there is nothing wrong with that. However, others, like me, live outside of the box. They may not know how much money will come in from month to month, but they suit up and show up to seize each day and work hard. Since turning my

life over to God, I believed that He would direct me into what He wanted me to do. I may make $1,200 one month and $10,000 the next, but I was happy doing what He wanted me to do.

20. **When God closes one door, He always opens another. But it's hell in the hallway.**
    a. It can take a lot of trust and patience to wait upon God to open that next door, but it will happen if we can see it through.
    b. When I was falsely accused of child molesting, it took about four years for God to open that next door. You would not be reading this if He hadn't opened that door, or if I had harmed myself or someone else due to behavior from rash impatience. It's never easy waiting on that door.

21. **When you drink from the water, you must remember the spring.**
    a. When we benefit from something, we must be thankful to the source.

22. **To go fast, you must go alone; but to go far, you must go together.**
    a. I love this saying. It indicates how we can excel in an endeavor when we don't need someone else's input or approval slowing us down. However, we will eventually run out of steam, become ill, or suffer an injury, and the progress we made will suspend, backslide, or end. When we proceed,

albeit more slowly, in a group, we have others to share the load, share ideas, and help with expansion and growth. There is also no guarantee that a group cannot succeed as quickly as going it alone.

23. **It is better to humble yourself before others than to be humbled by them.**
    a. I really dislike listening to others brag about themselves when there are so many others who could put them down very quickly.
    b. I heard about a little league baseball coach in a small town who barked at his children that he wasn't a loser, and he didn't train losers. But look at the big picture. If he is so great, why is he coaching little children in a small town with little competition?
    c. I once tested something I read in the Bible about humility. It said (not read, but said) it's better to sit lower down the table and be called up than to sit up near the head and be told to move down. I went to dinner with a group of martial artists after a workshop with an internationally acclaimed Hapkido instructor. I sat down by the entry-level black belts and family members. It wasn't long before the table master called me to come up and sit by him and told the person sitting there to move down and give me his seat. Part of

the reason for his success was his self-awareness and aggressive attitude, but he was very impressed by my humility of which he had no concept of achieving. In fact, this man is an example of going fast by going alone. But when he dies or retires, his empire will fall apart as he could never have a close relationship with those who succeeded in his program.

24. **We are known for our actions, not our intentions.**
   a. Have you meant to give someone a call to see how they were doing and then got busy and didn't make the call? I have. I even told someone I meant to call her, but I couldn't find her phone number. Her response was, "Yes, it's so hard to find a phone book when you need one."
   b. I intended (as a teenager) to go to college and change the world for the better, but there was half-price drinks every Tuesday at a local bar. That's just a joke. Actually, I had overloaded myself with classes in college and didn't want to put in the full time of study required to learn, so I decided to join the Marines and become disciplined. That's a whole other book. It's on the list of books to write.

25. **There is no winner in a fight.**
   a. This is one of my most quoted sayings in my classes, and it is my own personal quote. Here is my personal definition by explanation: I was a high-

ranking black belt, a very talented and extremely fast martial artist, and I was and still am deadly in street application of martial arts. If I were to have gotten into a street fight when I ran my school and was forced to hurt them, I would have lost because perception dictated that I should have been able to subdue him without hurting him. If I had lost, I would have lost because I couldn't defend myself.

b. This doesn't mean you should not defend yourself. You should. But if you are forced to hurt someone who tried to hurt you, that doesn't make you a winner; it makes you a survivor. The difference is in the attitude.

c. Competition is not a really a fight, it is a match. Mixed martial arts (MMA) is an exception. It's more of a brawl than a discipline. Someday it may develop into an art with discipline and even ethics. For now, however, I believe it should simply be called cage fighting.

26. **When searching for God, the first thing to know is He isn't the one lost.**

a. You don't need to go seek God at church (not to put down church), or at workshops and seminars, or in books and videos. You need only to stop, ask Him to reveal Himself to you, and believe that what happens next (maybe several days) is the answer of that prayer. What we need is a personal relationship with God through His son Jesus Christ (my personal belief). Personal! Not through a priest. Not through a husband. Not through a group of believers. Personal! Then you need to find a source, which will nourish your newly discovered spirituality. That's when you find a Bible study or church etc.

27. **If you believe yourself to be humble, then you're not.**
    a. Humility is something you don't usually see in yourself. If you have it, others will tell you. They may even brag on you to others. The goal is not to develop humility. It is to develop a kind and loving heart. By the way, there is a difference between being kind and being good. Goodness is *being* nice and kindness is *doing* nice.
    b. I knew a young martial artist who had just opened his own school and came to see me. He told me three times in that one conversation that I just wouldn't believe how humble he was. He also told me that he was world-ranked as a fighter. Two weeks later, I hosted a small tournament through my school. One of my black belts from Houston, who hadn't practiced in three years, happened to be in town and dropped by to see me that very morning. I told him to go over to the karate school and get a uniform and belt and come compete. I

matched him with the young humble champion as they were in the same age, skill, and weight range. My student beat him by an embarrassing score. He never came to see me again. By the way, I didn't judge that fight.

28. **Happiness is an illusion propagated by luxury.**
    a. When we meet people who live in opulence, we may naturally assume they are happy because they have been successful in life. But having a lot of stuff doesn't guarantee happiness. I once walked into a large beautiful home (when the wife had answered the door). Then I heard the husband scream from upstairs for her to get his breakfast ready. He had so much anger in his voice, and her face was full of sadness. When he saw me, his frown turned to a smile, and he greeted me.
    b. This quote may be an illusion itself because there are so many happy people who are wealthy, but the point of it is that most of us equate happiness with luxury.

29. **If you want to know a person's heart, look in their check register.**
    a. People spend their money on the things they enjoy most. I enjoy giving. Nothing pleases me more than to receive a large check because I can then take the first 10 percent assigned to God and give it to people I know who are struggling. Yes, I

give some to my little biker church, but most of it goes to the "big C"—church, the people.

30. **If no one else has done such a bad deed as you, why is there a name for it?**
    a. I have met a few adults and even children who believed they could never be forgiven for the things they have done. We have all failed to live up to the standards we feel are normal for an adjusted social life. But to believe you have committed such terrible acts that you could never receive forgiveness is to believe that you are greater than God.

31. **My life is none of my business.**
    a. If I have truly given my life to Christ, then what He does with it is none of my business. It is my business to suit up and show up for each new day that He allows me to have on this earth and make the best of it.
    b. I survived terminal cancer (see Stories). I believe it was so I could testify to people that
        i. Life isn't without bad things happening.
        ii. God can heal us if it is meant to be
            1. Sometimes God chooses to allow the sick to leave this life and be with Him in glory. Having suffered is a privilege to understand Jesus's suffering just a little better.

2. I believe the proverb "He who has a heart for children, I will heal him on his sickbed" is the reason I was healed of terminal cancer.

32. **The same raindrop which denies causing the flood will take credit for ending the drought.**
    a. I think we all tend to have a little nagging inside of us to deny fault in failures yet accept credit for positive things.

33. **There is a big difference between giving up and letting go.**
    a. Giving up is a sign of weakness to quit trying.
    b. Letting go is to quit trying to get our own way by fighting everything and everyone, and letting God be in control.

34. **There is no spoon.**
    a. This earthly life is not the real life. The real life, to which we should aspire, is the eternal life with God. This *entire life* is just one breath in eternal life. Live one day at a time with the real life, eternal life, in mind on how you choose to behave and believe today.

35. **You can't give away what you ain't got.**
    a. It's good to want to help others, but you need to have the knowledge and/or experience in order to do so. I witnessed a car salesman buy a video on how to sign someone to a karate contract, and the

next thing you know, he was a karate master with his own karate school. It didn't last, but he made money and then disappeared.

36. **Don't believe everything you think.**
    a. We all have thoughts about what others are thinking when we, in truth, don't have any idea. Some people will do this so much that they actually believe the other person thinks that way. Have you ever seen two people talking across the room, and when they looked up and at you, you assumed they were talking about you? Did you get angry? That is how misunderstandings can start fights.

37. **Happiness isn't getting what you want; it's accepting what you get.**
    a. When I was a young man, I just knew that if I had a new car, or a new girlfriend, or a new house, then I'd be happy. When I was able to be content with what I had, that was when I began to feel comfortable in my own skin.

38. **The storms of life are never in the forecast.**
    a. A car wreck, a robbery and/or murder, an illness. These can all happen in a moment and change our lives forever, or even end our lives. We need to love, honor, cherish, and forgive each other constantly throughout each day. I pray for my enemies as well as my friends. I want them to receive healing and good fortune. Mean people cannot be blessed

until they are first broken. I don't want people to get theirs on judgment day. I would rather God break them through divorce or publicly revealed alcoholism and then see them be healed.

39. **Two ding-a-lings don't make a bell.**
    a. The Bible says if one blind man leads another, they will both fall into a ditch. When we need help, we should seek it from someone with the knowledge and training to move us forward in the direction we want.
    b. I've seen people buy a book and a videotape on martial arts and train themselves. You can hang a bag in your garage and in a couple of months have some pretty good scraping abilities. But you will not learn all of the little nuances that accompany learning martial arts correctly, thereby mastering your own body.

40. **Those who matter, don't mind; and those who mind, don't matter.**
    a. A bodyguard for a dignitary overseas once heard this discussion over a dinner. The wife of one dignitary, noticing her forks were improperly aligned, told the host that it must be difficult finding good help outside of our country. He remarked with the above statement. People who really are important will be discussing delicate issues over dinner, not worrying about proper dining protocol and procedure.

41. **It's better to be a bird than a turtle.**
    a. Watching a beach on the East Coast, a man noticed the turtles hatching in the sand and slowly making their way to the ocean as birds snatched up the struggling babies for easy meals. His conclusion was that it is better to follow your dreams with action rather than to follow the slow-paced behavior of safe normal human movement. I didn't want a job; I wanted a career, and I wanted it to be what and where God wanted me.

42. **Sometimes we need to take the cotton out of our ears and put it in our mouth.**
    a. We have two ears and one mouth, therefore we should listen twice as much as we talk. The Bible says to be slow to speak and slower to anger. I used to find myself talking on and on about things of which I had a little knowledge and a lot of opinion. I just loved to hear the sound of my own voice. I think a lot of people have this problem.

43. **I'd rather be happy than right.**
    a. Fighting a long drawn-out battle just to prove I was right (to me) is not worth the trouble. I'd rather just forget about it and move on. You can't unring a bell.
    b. After I was released from being held in jail due to a false accusation, I was told I should go after the city and the media for the lies told about

me. But what was done was done. The only ones I did consider going after was a homeschooling group whose president told their members that I was guilty.

44. **Everyone has life, but few really know how to live it.**
    a. When I was a teenager, I was in such a hurry to go nowhere. Age eventually teaches most of us to slow down and just enjoy the moment. I'm just thankful that I didn't spend the majority of my life on a barstool.

45. **Every decision has either a result or a consequence.**
    a. Positive choices result in positive actions. Negative behavior and poor choices have consequences. Drunkenness can result in prison terms for intoxicated manslaughter with a car or rape and unwanted pregnancy, often not even knowing who had fathered the child.

46. **You may be the only Bible some people will ever read.**
    a. If you are a religious person and are one of the few who live with your belief in your heart, I say amen. Most people claim to and try to be religious, but their greed and vanity scatters their message rather than carrying it to the lost.

47. **A tranquil mind is the first requisite for good judgment.**
    a. A peaceful life without a crowded mind gives clarity for sober judgment when making decisions or giving advice. Are you sober-minded?

48. **Peace of mind cannot be bought at the expense of others.**
    a. Taking advantage of others to make yourself feel better will come back to haunt you. It's better to do without than to harm God's children.
49. **Acceptance is the key to all my problems.**
    a. I must first accept that what is happening in life is, in fact, happening before I can successfully turn it over to God for Him to handle.
50. **He who conquers himself is greater than he who conquers a city.**
    a. When we learn to control our own emotions, fears, insecurities, and character defects, we will truly have accomplished something great.
51. **It's hard to remember your main mission was to drain the swamp when you're up to your ass in alligators.**
    a. We can get so sidetracked by problems that are stumbling blocks to accomplishing our designated tasks. Sometimes we may need to ask for help. Asking for help is not a sign of weakness, it's a sign of intelligent reasoning to reach the intended goal.

Appendix I

The Seven Deadly Sins

1. **Pride**. Excessive belief in one's own abilities.
2. **Envy**. Desire for other's possessions, traits, status, or abilities.
3. **Gluttony**. Inordinate desire to consume more than that which one required.
4. **Lust**. Inordinate craving for the pleasures of the body.
5. **Anger**. Manifested in the individual who spurns love and opts for wrath.
6. **Greed**. Desire for material wealth or gain.
7. **Sloth**. Avoidance of physical or spiritual work.

Department of Justice Figures

➢ Approximately 95 percent of the victims of domestic violence are women.

- Every nine seconds in the United States, a woman is assaulted and beaten.
- Four million women a year are assaulted by their partners.
- In the United States, a woman is more likely to be assaulted, injured, raped, or killed by a male partner than by any other type of assailant.
- Every day, four women are murdered by boyfriends or husbands.
- Prison terms for women killing their husbands in self-defense are twice as long than for husbands killing their wives in anger.
- Ninety-three percent of women who killed their mates had been battered by them.
- Sixty-seven percent of women who killed their mates did so to protect themselves and their children at the moment of the murder.
- Twenty-five percent of all crime is wife assault.
- Seventy percent of men who batter their partners either sexually or physically abuse their children.
- Domestic violence is the number one cause of emergency room visits by women.
- Family violence kills as many women every five years as the total number of Americans who died in the Vietnam War.

Office on Violence

- In America, one in four women, and one in thirteen men will experience domestic violence in their lifetime.
- Each day, on average, three women die as a result of domestic violence.
- Stalkers victimize approximately 2.53 million women each year in the United States.
- Domestic violence-related stalking is the most common type of stalking and the most dangerous.
- One million women in the United States are raped every year.

Current statistics on rape and sexual assault of college-age students and nonstudents can be found on the website of the Bureau of Justice Statistics (www.bjs.gov).

Current statistics on human trafficking (which is mainly abductions of young females sold into sex slavery) can be found on the website of the Federal Bureau of Investigation (www.fbi.gov).

Appendix II

REVIEW YOUR KNOWLEDGE by answering the questions below. Remember, in order to use these skills, you must be sure you know them. This review is for *your* knowledge.

In the first set of questions, circle the most correct number. College scholarships can be granted:

1. Only through sports
2. For good grades
3. Only if you are rich

Wearing the backpack high on the back:

1. Looks uncool
2. Causes lower back injuries
3. Puts less strain on the back muscles

Intimidation is:

1. A normal emotion
2. Not a normal emotion
3. Depends how you use it

Status is:

1. Okay if you don't hurt people
2. The number one most important senior trait
3. Only for seniors

If a guy buys a girl a nice dinner:

1. She owes him sex
2. She owes him a kiss
3. Neither 1 or 2

If your date is forward:

1. Break their arm
2. Just smile and go with it
3. Start talking about your parents

Emotional boundaries are:

1. Both external and internal
2. Your friends feelings
3. The property line around your house

Showing your undershorts or bra straps:

1. Is part of society and people need to get over it
2. Shows a lack of purity in dress
3. Is only okay if they are clean

Organizing at home requires:

1. Studying, with no breaks, until you are caught up
2. A drop spot
3. Studying only in your room

When you get the test:

1. Answer the questions you know first
2. Do your best
3. Only answer the questions in the order they are listed

A defensive mental edge is:

1. The instinct to sense when an attacker is near
2. The ability to recognize potentially abusive behavior
3. The trained ability to read negative thoughts of others

Children should be allowed to:

1. Switch sports after participating for an agreed time
2. Choose a sport from those selected by the parent
3. Both 1 and 2.

Mind reading is:

1. Believing you know what others think
2. Part of a defensive mental edge
3. A type of spider sense achieved through martial arts training

True / False

1. _____ Compliments are specific and sincere.
2. _____ When accepting "no" as an answer, the first thing to do is look away from the person's eyes.
3. _____ After a breakup, don't make hurtful comments about the other.
4. _____ The first thing to do when apologizing is look at the person.
5. _____ Only shake hands with people if they stand.
6. _____ Always smile when talking on the phone.
7. _____ You should always remove your hat when entering someone's home.
8. _____ If you call someone and they aren't home, call back every ten minutes.
9. _____ It's okay to wear your hat at the dinner table.
10. _____ Learning these skills is useless.

11. _____ Every nine seconds in the United States, a woman is assaulted and beaten.
12. _____ A woman who kills her husband in the self-defense of her children will go to prison for twice as long as a man who beats his wife to death in anger.

What I found most helpful about the information in this book was:

_____
_____
_____
_____
_____
_____

What I enjoyed most about this book was:

_____
_____
_____
_____
_____
_____

Test Answers (p. 128):

1. True
2. False
3. False
4. True
5. True
6. True
7. True
8. True
9. True

Test Answers (p. 200):

1. Betrays
2. Control
3. Relationship
4. Bribe
5. Status
6. Compliment
7. Control

Other Books by Danny Passmore

Positive Defensive Behavior by Danny Passmore

Watch for these upcoming books:

The Nice Ninjas Training Manual
The *Rance Robinson Adventure Series* for kids.

All stories based on real life adventures and experiences of Danny Passmore:

Rance Robinson in the Forbidden Zone (of the original *Planet of the Apes* movie)

Rance Robinson in the Secret Submarine Base (on the Italian coast)

Rance Robinson in the Sahara Desert (the plight of the Saharawi)

Rance Robinson in the Gulf of Mexico (the biggest fish a boy could catch)

Rance Robinson in the Underwater Explorer (800 feet below the sea)

Rance Robinson and the Dolphins (an ocean ride with Danny the Dolphin)

Notes

Phone Numbers